T0236416

Series Editors

W. Hansmann
W. T. Hewitt
W. Purgathofer

B. Arnaldi

G. Hégron (eds.)

Computer Animation
and Simulation '98

Proceedings of the Eurographics Workshop
in Lisbon, Portugal,
August 31 – September 1, 1998

Eurographics

SpringerWienNewYork

Dr. Bruno Arnaldi
IRISA, Rennes, France

Dr. Gérard Hégron
Ecole des Mines de Nantes, Nantes, France

This work is subject to copyright.
All rights are reserved, whether the whole or part of the material is concerned, specifically those of translation, reprinting, re-use of illustrations, broadcasting, reproduction by photo-copying machines or similar means, and storage in data banks.

© 1999 Springer-Verlag/Wien
Printed in Austria

Typesetting: Camera ready by authors
Printing: Druckerei Novographic, A-1238 Wien
Binding: Fa. Papyrus, A-1100 Wien

Graphic design: Ecke Bonk

Printed on acid-free and chlorine-free bleached paper

SPIN: 10708927

With 82 Figures

ISSN 0946-2767
ISBN 3-211-83257-2 Springer-Verlag Wien New York

Preface

The 9th Eurographics workshop on Animation and Simulation was held on August 31st - September 1st, 1998, at INESC Lisbon. The workshop was chaired by Bruno Arnaldi (IRISA Rennes, France) and Gérard Hégron (Ecole des Mines de Nantes, France). The local organizer Mário Rui Gomes (INESC Lisbon, Portugal) notably contributed to provide a harmonious environment. The main theme of this seventh workshop was centered on *Virtual Reality versus Animation and Simulation: from real time animation/simulation to physical perception of virtual environments*. About twenty participants attended the workshop, representing eight countries: France, Spain, Austria, Switzerland, Ireland, Portugal, Germany and USA. The Program Committee selected eight papers among submitted papers. Thirteen minutes of presentation and fifteen minutes discussion time per paper was also planned; this approach succeeded in creating a stimulating exchange atmosphere during the two days.

Four sessions have been organized :

Applications : in this session, two papers were presented, the first one deals with the use of simulation in natural desasters prevention while the second one concerns dynamic light sources for radiosity environments

natural simulation : the first paper of this session presents works on real time behavioral simulation from psychological studies, the second one deals with identification of motion for living beeing.

Interaction : the first paper presents a method for interactively animate solid using displacement contraints and the second paper presents the modeling of objects for interactive virtual human tasks.

Modelling : the first paper presents assisted articulation of polygonal models while the second one describes STIGMA, a 4-dimensional modeller for animation.

I wish to thank the local organisator Mário Rui Gomes and his colleagues at INSC Lisbon for their help before and during the workshop.

Bruno Arnaldi
Gérard Hégron

International Programme committee

- Bruno Arnaldi (France)
- Norman Badler (USA)
- Robert Bodenheimer (USA)
- Ronan Boulic (Switzerland)
- Michael Cohen (USA)
- Sabine Coquillart (France)
- Marie-Paule Cani-Gascuel (France)
- Gerard Hegron (France)
- Annie Luciani (France)
- Nadia Magnenat-Thalmann (Switzerland)
- Daniel Thalmann (Switzerland)
- Michiel Van de Panne (Canada)
- Kees van Overveld (The Netherlands)
- Phil Willis (UK)

Contents

Contents

Contents

Simulating Landslides for Natural Disaster Prevention

Jean-Dominique Gascuel, Marie-Paule Cani-Gascuel,
Mathieu Desbrun[†]

iMAGIS[‡]-GRAVIR UMR C5527 / IMAG

BP 53, F-38041 Grenoble cedex 09, France

Eric Leroi, Carola Mirgon

Bureau de Recherches Géologiques et Minières,

Direction de la Recherche,

117 avenue de Luminy, BP 167, 13276 Marseille, France

Contact: `Jean-Dominique.Gascuel@imag.fr`

Abstract

The simulation of landslide hazards is a key point in the prevention of natural disasters, since it enables to compute risk maps and helps to design protection works. We present a 3D simulator that handles both rock-falls and mud-flows. The terrain model is built from geological and vegetation maps, superimposed on a DEM. Since the exact elevation of the terrain is unknown at the rock's scale, the simulator uses a series of stochastic simulations, where low scale geometry is slightly randomized at each impact, to compute an envelop of risk areas. Computations are optimized using an implicit formulation of surfaces and a space-time adaptive algorithm for animating the particle system that represents the mud flow.

1 Introduction

Computing trajectories of rocky blocks or viscous mud falling or flowing down slope is a preoccupation for many engineering firms that have to establish safety perimeters, or must design protection works. In the area of geophysics, only a few simulation codes are available for such work and even rarer are those that tackle the three dimensional aspect of simulation. On the other hand, Computer Graphics "physically-based animation" systems are now able to simulate a vast range of phenomena, from rigid bodies to viscous liquids interacting with a dynamic environment.

[†] Currently at: Department of Computer Science, Caltech, USA

[‡] iMAGIS is a joint project of CNRS, INRIA, Institut National Polytechnique de Grenoble and Université Joseph Fourier.

1.1 Background

Performing landslides simulations for preventing natural disasters is a difficult task. One of the main reason is the lack of precision on the data: the available resolution for terrain elevation is usually too low compared with the size of the rocks falling down slope, leading to important imprecisions on bouncing directions ; local vegetation should be taken into account since it plays an important part on friction coefficients at each impact; moreover, the exact characteristics of the rocks or the mud that are going to flow down slope are unknown as well. A solution is to perform a large number of slightly different simulations, which stochastic changes of parameters at each impact, and use the envelop of all the computed trajectories to delimit risk areas. However, this approach yields drastic constraints on the efficiency of simulations.

As a result, computer simulations have not been used much in the area of geophysics. Most existing simulators (eg. [8, 16, 12]) are based on 2D profiles of terrains instead of 3D elevation models. They compute trajectories of spherical blocks (i.e., circles since computations are performed in 2D) for which translational and rotational velocities after each bounce are computed by multiplying incident velocities by empirical "collision parameters", that are calibrated using a least square fitting over measured real cases. Computations can be achieved quite efficiently, but the results really suffer from a lack of precision: mechanical properties of materials are only coarsely approximated, and no stress-deformation law is used for instance. Moreover, since computations are only made on a set of 2D profiles, results (ie. envelops of risk areas) may be wrong compared to what would happen in the real 3-dimensional environment, depending on the specific geometry of the terrain.

To the authors knowledge, there has been no work specifically devoted to landslides simulations from the Computer Graphics community. However, models for soft grounds interacting with dynamic objects such as vehicles or human bodies have already been designed [3, 18]. In the first of these works, the large-scale plastic (nonlinear) deformations of the ground are modeled by a coarse array of masses that move in 3D, linked together and to the under-ground by visco-plastic interactions. The small-scale linear deformations are modeled by a finer array of masses moving vertically, according to the "pin-screen" paradigm. Colliding objects interact with both grids. This results into very realistic images of footprints left by vehicle wheels, that include small bulges around compressed areas. In [18], the same visual effect is produced, under the hypothesis of constant volume deformations, by transporting to neighboring regions ground matter inter-penetrating with the feet of synthetic runners.

As will be shown below, our choices for the ground model are quite different, since our aim is not to produce nice footprints left by rocks falling down slope, but rather to provide an efficient simulation of rock trajectories from ground stress-deformation laws provided by geophysicists. In our case, only ground compression under collision is computed, since it affects the subsequent motion of the falling rock.

1.2 Overview

This paper presents a landslide simulator that performs 3D dynamic simulations of rock-falls and mud-flows. Based on both geo-mechanical data and physically-based animation algorithms, it handles various models that interact together during simulations such as elasto-plastic material for the ground, rigid solid for the rocks, and viscous liquid for the mud. Moreover, it tackles the problem of computational efficiency :

- Only regions of the ground where impact may take place at the next time step are simulated. A local re-sampling provides a representation of the ground at a smaller scale in these regions of interest.

- Implicit formulations of surfaces are used to accelerate collision detection and to compute ground deformations.

- Mud-flows are computed using an adaptive simulation, where the number and size of particles that sample the mud are adapted over time according to the oc-curring deformations (many particles are used in areas that deform much, while only a few of them is used in stable regions).

The remainder of this paper develops as follows: Section 2 explains how we process geophysics data for building the 3D model of the terrain. Computation of trajectories for rocks falling or sliding down slopes is detailed in Section 3. Muds-flows simulation is described in Section 4. Section 5 concludes and discusses work in progress.

2 Modeling geological data

This section introduces the geological concepts used throughout this paper. They differ somehow from what is usually found in the Computer Graphics literature, since we must share a common language and understanding with the geophysics community.

2.1 Geological data

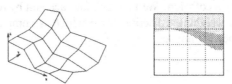

Figure 1: Digital Geology: The elevation model (DEM, on the left), and lithology or vegetation maps (right)

Digital Elevation Models (DEM) (see figure 1) give the altitude of the terrains on a 2D grid. Usually, the resolution is low in comparison with the simulations that will take place: a step of a few tens of meters is common. To that altitude map, we super-impose a lithological (such as granite, swamp, etc) and a vegetation map.

The lithology is used to compute how the ground deforms during a collision. Fig-ure 2 present a typical collision cycle of a rock against a typical elasto-plastic material "with strain". A collision process takes three steps:

1. Elastic compression: when the rock starts to deform the ground, the ground response force is a linear function of the penetration.

2. Plastic deformation: at a given pressure level, the internal structure of the ground is modified. The response force suddenly changes of slope, since the energy is mainly spent in deformation.

3. Elastic decompression: the response force decreases linearly *from the maximal penetration point*, and with *a higher slope* because of ground stress.

The dashed integral in the figure represents the energy loss during the collision. The difference between the cycle start and the cycle end gives the footprint that the rock will leave onto the ground. Geophysicists usually take parameters of stress cycles from existing tables, or measure them on the field.

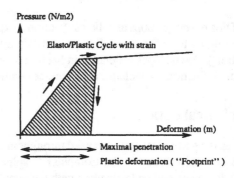

Figure 2: A typical stress cycle. The dashed area represents the energy loss during a collision.

Usually, natural terrains are not bare. Their vegetal cover plays an important part in the loss of energy during a collision. We take this into account by defining an "energy deperdition" coefficient weighing a friction force which is computed as a quadratic function of the rock's speed at impact.

2.2 Ground model

In order to have a continuous description of the terrain, we must interpolate the DEM data. We use a bilinear interpolation (see figure 3a) of the various data known at each node of the DEM grid (altitude, elasto/plastic coefficients, vegetation friction, etc.) to sample the ground at a smaller scale. The refined ground model can be seen as a bidimensional array of "pistons" modeling the deformations of cylindrical samples of the soil in the normal direction to the local ground surface (see figure 3b).

During computations, each piston will store the local stress history needed to compute plastic deformations and response according to the given stress cycle. Geo-physicists use to neglect transversal transport of matter, which is difficult to quantify. Moreover, we are only interested here into modeling the compression of the soil under the falling rock, which will affect the dynamics of the rock after the impact: modeling local bulges

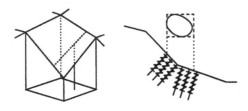

Figure 3: Digital Elevation Model (DEM): (a) bilinear interpolation of elevations; (b) and the model for pistons carpet below the rock.

around compressed areas as was done in previous Computer Graphics works on footprints [3, 18] is not needed for our application. In consequence, each piston deforms and responds to collisions independently from its neighbors. It applies to colliding objects axial response forces, normal to the deformed ground surface.

Storing and simulating at each time step the whole ground at the smallest scale would consume too much memory and computational time. We rather perform a local adaptation of the ground's *level of detail* during computations: a fine grid is computed by caching the ground data only over a small "region of interest", defined as the vertical projection of the rock's axis-parallel bounding box. We call this region the "piston's carpet", as pistons are really computed only in this area. When the rock moves, rows and columns of pistons are removed or added to the adequate side of the carpet, thus taking benefits of temporal coherence. By this means, we focus computations only where needed.

As a result, footprints left by the rocks onto the ground, which are computed during impacts since they are essential for finding the ground's response, are not updated anymore when the rock moves down-slope to another region of interest. This greatly accelerates computations, since the number of pistons to process is proportional to the size of the falling rock, rather than to the size of the ground data-base.

3 Trajectory simulation for rocky blocks

3.1 Model for the rocks

In our simulations, rocks are rigid solids defined by an implicit surface [2] whose sample points are stored in a local frame. Each rock is provided with a mass and an inertia tensor, and is animated with usual dynamic laws of motion.

In some cases, modeling large rocky blocks fracturing into smaller ones may be useful. Our approach is to model these large blocks as a set of rigid parts linked together by geometric constraints [10]. When internal constraint forces exceed a given threshold, the constraint is suppressed, so the block breaks into pieces (see Figure 4).

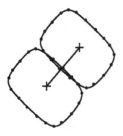

Figure 4: Rock fracture can be modeled using pre-fractured solids linked by breakable constraints.

3.2 Air friction during rock-fall

In addition to gravity, we model air-friction during rock flight phases. The equation we use is:

$$\overrightarrow{airFriction} = \frac{1}{2}\rho C_x \int \|V\| \vec{V} \cdot \vec{n}\, dS$$

where $\frac{\vec{V}}{\|\vec{V}\|} \cdot \vec{n}\, dS$ is a surface element of the rock, seen from the air flow, ρ the air density, and $0 < C_x < 1$ the drag coefficient (equals to 0.1 for a heavy sphere).

3.3 Collisions with the ground

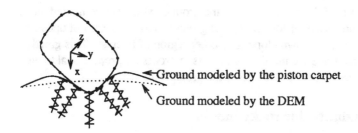

Figure 5: A rock interacting with pistons of the refined ground model

We compute collision detection and response within three steps, as in [11]:

1. We take benefits of the implicit formulation for the rock to optimize collision detection by testing each piston's surface point against the rock implicit function.

2. When a collision is detected, we model the rock's footprint on the ground by compressing along its axis each piston which penetrates the rock. Using the implicit formulation of the rock, the exact new locations of these pistons are computed through binary search.

3. Each piston computes a response force in the direction of the normal to the deformed ground according to its new length and to its current state (elastic compression, plastic deformation, or decompression states). It also stores the new state to be used at the next time step.

4. Normal response forces and viscous friction forces weighted by the vegetation coefficient are added to the set of external actions to be applied to the rock up at the next time step.

3.4 Fast Bounce mode

Although the simulation process is quite fast (almost real-time on a low end workstation), it is sometime useful to simulate a hundred of trajectories in a few seconds, just to have an idea of a parameter change, for instance. Hence, a fast simulation mode was added to the simulator. The basic idea is to use a rough collision model, based on impulse and a single-point collision detection. The collision processing algorithm then becomes:

1. Test if the center point of the bottom face of the rock's bounding box is below the ground,

2. Move the rock up so that no more collision occurs, and generate an impulse at the collision point. The impulse is such that the speed after collision is reflected by the ground surface, and takes into account an arbitrary energy loss coefficient.

This energy loss coefficient could be chosen by geophysicists in relation with simpler simulation models, or tuned to match simulation results from the full rock-ground interaction model. In the first case, they could check if the new detailed simulation accurately match old well known but limited models. In the later case, they could fine tune the accelerated mode on a simple and well known configuration, then use it as a coarse model for complex configurations.

3.5 Stochastic Simulation and Results

As said before, the detailed geometry of the ground is not perfectly known. A randomization of various simulation parameters enables to have different trajectories for a block, and to assert hazard zones by stochastic simulations. But since the occurring contacts are not punctual (contact forces are integrated over a whole contact area), randomization of the terrain should have some spatial coherence (see figure 6). If they don't, summing over the rock's surface will average out the randomness added to the surface normals.

We use a Perlin[17] noise model, with a frequency of the order of the rock's size.

$$
\begin{aligned}
A &= Tab[Hash(E(\lambda x), E(\lambda y))] \\
B &= Tab[Hash(E(\lambda x) + 1, E(\lambda y))] \\
C &= Tab[Hash(E(\lambda x), E(\lambda y) + 1)] \\
D &= Tab[Hash(E(\lambda x) + 1, E(\lambda y) + 1)] \\
Perlin_0(x, y) &= BilinearInterpol(A, B, C, D, frac(\lambda x), frac(\lambda y))
\end{aligned}
$$

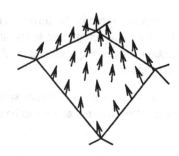

Figure 6: Because the force is integrated over a large contact area, the geometric randomness added for the stochastic simulation should have spatial coherence.

$$Perlin(x, y) = Perlin_0(x, y) + \frac{1}{2}Perlin_0(2*x, 2*y)$$
$$+ \frac{1}{4}Perlin_0(4*x, 4*y) + \cdots$$

Where $E(x)$ is the integral part, and $frac(x) = x - E(X)$ the fractional part of a number x.

The basic idea is to initialize once for each simulation a random array $Tab[]$, and to have an hash function that maps the noise parameters (here the x and y space coordinates) to an index in that array. Four values are taken from that table, and bilinearly interpolated to have the base $Perlin_0$ noise. The base frequency is given by the parameter λ, and higher frequency noise are usually added by summing scaled $Perlin_0$ noise functions.

Gathering simulation data

To gather simulation data, a "*statistical map*" can be attached to any DEM, representing various parameters: blocks velocity, altitude, height over the ground, energy loss by friction, energy loss by ground deformation, etc. These data are saved for later analysis, or used to display statistical information on the ground, using arbitrary color scales on a vertically projected texture map.

4 Simulating mud-flows

4.1 Modeling mud with smoothed particles

The second typical phenomena in landslides is mud flowing down slope. Viscous fluids such as mud are difficult to simulate since conventional simulation methods as finite elements hardly cope with large deformations and changes of topology. Eulerian approaches, that consist in discretizing space into voxels and then computing what flows in and out each voxel [9] would not be convenient here, since interactions with obstacles which are not necessarily aligned with voxels need to be computed. Physically-based particle systems, such as those used in [15, 19, 20, 14, 7] seem a better approach for our case.

Our approach relies on the "smoothed particles" model introduced in [4]. The main feature of smoothed particles is to model materials governed by a macroscopic *state equation*. It defines the global behavior of the material independently of the sampling rate. Since real mud-flows may consist into large set of heterogeneous materials (including small rocks, trees, etc), no precise mechanical model could model such a behavior accurately. Defining a macroscopic behavior, designed or fitted on data, is then convenient. The state equation governs the evolution of a *pressure* field P inside the substance. Conservative internal forces, called "pressure forces", are proportional to the gradient of pressure [1]. These forces are combined with dissipative forces that model internal friction inside the deformable body.

Our macroscopic model for mud flows is a viscous substance that comes back to a constant volume when no external force is applied. To simulate this behavior, we set the state equation to [4]:

$$P = k(\rho - \rho_0) \tag{1}$$

This generates pressure forces that tend to restore a rest density ρ_0 when the current density ρ has become too high or too low. The parameter k in equation (1) controls the strength of density recovering, and is thus analogous to a stiffness parameter.

This equation is a simplified version of the state equation for fluids flows in isothermic media:

$$\rho = \rho_0 e^{-c(P_0 - P)}$$

where variations of the compressibility $c = \frac{1}{\rho}\frac{\partial \rho}{\partial P}$ depending of pressure have been neglected (i.e. $c = c_0$, the compressibility at reference pressure P_0), and $c_0|P_0 - P|$ supposed sufficiently small.

During a simulation, the matter is sampled by particles, or sample points, representing a small mass distribution around them. Attraction/repulsion forces between particles are derived from the state equation as being proportional to the gradient of pressure, thus yielding different approximations of the same behavior whatever the sampling resolution. Then, motion is obtained through integration of forces over time.

Modeling mud-flows with changing mass as in [12] is easy with our model: we just have to position some extra material on the terrain. During the simulation, the flow may entrain some of this ground material while some of the flow particles may be stopped by friction.

4.2 Adaptive simulation

To increase efficiency while maintaining a given accuracy, the number and size of particles sampling the mud-flow are adaptively modified during computations. Local fission and fusions of particles are automatically generated in order to optimize computation while keeping a desired accuracy. As a result, fewer and larger particles are used in stable areas while refinements occur where the substance undergoes deformation.

More precisely, during an animation:

- A particle subdivides if the local difference of pressure with its neighbors compared to the particle size exceeds a given threshold.

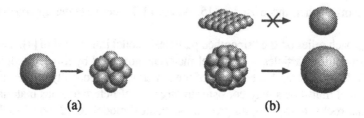

(a)   (b)

Figure 7: Adaptive animation scheme: (a) Particles are divided into smaller ones where high deformations are taking place. (b) Particles merge in stable areas.

- A group of particles merge into one particle when the volume they sample is almost spherical and their difference of pressure is under another threshold (see Figure 7) .

As our deformation model relies on a pressure proportional to the local mass density variation, these criteria ensure a better sampling where motion is about to occur, while it cuts down computation where it is stable. Particles are also simulated with individual time steps that are computed from their size and from stability criteria such as Courant condition, further improving efficiency while ensuring stability [6].

4.3   Results

A frame from an adaptive simulation of a mud-like substance is shown in Figure 9 (a). The adaptive simulation is about 4 times faster than the non-adaptive one computed with the finest particle's scale. Displaying particles as spheres gives a good idea of the subdivision/fusion process. In practice, we often coat the adaptive particle system with an *active implicit surface* [5], to get a smooth rendering. This active surface filters the changes of granularity of the internal particle system as it tracks a mass density isovalue while simulating a surface tension. It also yields an efficient polygonization, since it is computed as an iso-surface of a discrete field stored in a grid.

5   Conclusion

The presented rock-fall simulator is developed in C++ ($\approx$10.000 lines), and interfaced with the *Tcl* scripting language. It has already been used for an expertise. The *Motif* interface is being adapted to be usable by geophysicists, and we are currently calibrating our simulations using video-recorded rock falls in a stone quarry. The mud-flow simulator is still in progress: the base simulation model is fully functional, and integration into the geophysic framework of the first simulator is currently on the way.

Future works includes the modeling of snow and lava, which requires to add temperature in our state equation.

Acknowledgments: The authors would like to thank Frederic Pontarollo and Jocelyne Leroy for their contributions to this project.

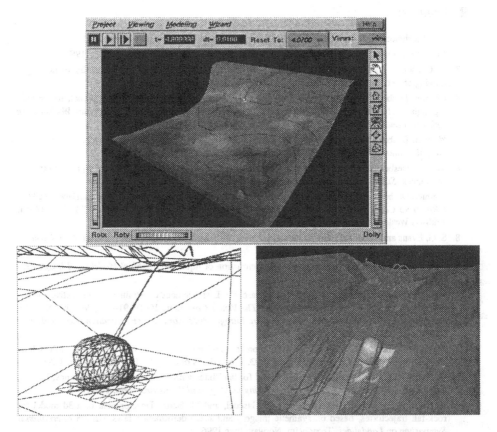

Figure 8: Top: Snapshot of the simulator. Left: a closup to the trajectory of a bloc (in red), with the *piston's carpet* mesh in yellow. Note the plastic deformation of the ground. Right: a set of trajectories. The ground is colored in cyan by the energy loss due to ground collision.

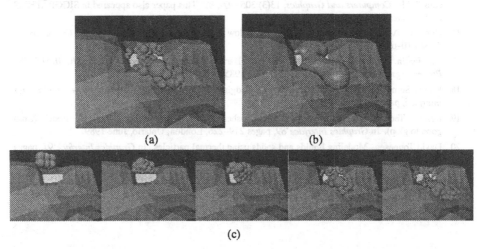

(a)

(b)

(c)

Figure 9: Mud-like substance flowing over a dam: (a) Adaptive particles displayed as spheres. (b) Particles coated with an active implicit surface. (c) The whole animation sequence.

References

1. G.K Batchelor. *An Introduction to Fluid Dynamics*. Cambridge University Press, 1973.

2. Jules Bloomenthal, editor. *Introduction to Implicit Surfaces*. Morgan Kaufmann, July 1997.

3. B. Chanclou, A. Luciani, and A. Habibi. Physical models of loose soils dynamically marked by a moving object. In *Computer Animation Conference 1996*, pages –, June 1996.

4. Mathieu Desbrun and Marie-Paule Cani-Gascuel. Smoothed particles: A new approach for animating highly deformable bodies. In Springer Computer Science, editor, *7th Eurographics Workshop on Animation and Simulation*, pages 61–76, Poitiers, France, September 1996.

5. Mathieu Desbrun and Marie-Paule Cani-Gascuel. Active implicit surface for computer animation. In *Graphics Interface (GI'98) Proceedings*, Vancouver, Canada, June 1998.

6. Mathieu Desbrun and Marie-Paule Cani-Gascuel. Space-time adaptive simulation of highly deformable substances. *Submitted for publication*, pages –, 1998.

7. Mathieu Desbrun and Marie-Paule Gascuel. Animating soft substances with implicit surfaces. In *SIGGRAPH 95 Conference Proceedings*, Annual Conference Series, pages 287–290. ACM SIGGRAPH, Addison Wesley, August 1995. Los Angeles, CA.

8. S. G. Evans and O. Hungr. The assessment of rockfall hazard at the base of talus slopes. *Can. Geotech. J.*, 30:620–636, 1993.

9. Nick Foster and Dimitri Metaxas. Realistic animation of liquids. *Graphical Models and Image Processing*, 58(5):471–483, 1996.

10. Jean-Dominique Gascuel and Marie-Paule Gascuel. Displacement constraints for interactive modeling and animation of articulated structures. *The Visual Computer*, 10(4):191–204, March 1994. An early version of this paper appeared in the *Third Eurographics Workshop on Animation and Simulation*, Cambridge, UK, Sept 92.

11. Marie-Paule Gascuel. An implicit formulation for precise contact modeling between flexible solids. *Computer Graphics*, 27:313–320, August 1993. Proceedings of SIGGRAPH'93 (Anaheim, CA).

12. O. Hungr and S. G. Evans. A dynamic model for landslides with changing mass. In Marinos, Koukis, Tsiambaos, and Stoumgras, editors, *Engineering Geology and the Environment*, 1997.

13. E. Leroi, F. Pontarollo, J-D. Gascuel, M-P Gascuel, and M. Bour. Development of a 3d model for rock-fall trajectories, based on synthetic imagery and stress-deformation laws. In *7th International Symposium on Landslides*, Trondheim, Norway, June 1996.

14. Annie Luciani, Stéphane Jimenez, Olivier Raoult, Claude Cadoz, and Jean-Loup Florens. A unified view of multitude behaviour, flexibility, plasticity, and fractures: balls, bubbles and agglomerates. In *IFIP WG 5.10 Working Conference*, Tokyo, Japan, April 1991.

15. Gavin Miller and Andrew Pearce. Globular dynamics: A connected particle system for animating viscous fluids. *Computers and Graphics*, 13(3):305–309, 89. This paper also appeared in SIGGRAPH'89 Course notes number 30.

16. Hungr O. A model for runout analysis of rapid flow slides, debris flows and avalanches. *Can. Geotech. J.*, 32:610–623, 1995.

17. Ken Perlin. An image synthesizer. In B. A. Barsky, editor, *Computer Graphics (SIGGRAPH '85 Proceedings)*, volume 19, pages 287–296, July 1985.

18. Robert Sumner, James O'Brien, and Jessica Hodgins. Animating sand, mud, and snow. In *Graphics Interface*, pages –, June 1998.

19. Demetri Terzopoulos, John Platt, and Kurt Fleisher. Heating and melting deformable models (from goop to glop). In *Graphics Interface'89*, pages 219–226, London, Ontario, June 1989.

20. David Tonnesen. Modeling liquids and solids using thermal particles. In *Graphics Interface'91*, pages 255–262, Calgary, AL, June 1991.

A Dynamic Light Sources Algorithm for Radiosity Environments

Gonzalo Besuievsky
Xavier Pueyo

(gonzalo|xavier)@ima.udg.es
Institut d'Informàtica i Aplicacions
Universitat de Girona
Campus de Montilivi, E 17071 Girona

Abstract

Global illumination solutions are required when dealing with realistic animation. This paper presents a new algorithm for dealing with dynamic light sources in animated radiosity environments. The algorithm computes in an efficient way the direct illumination of animated lights, which in general is an expensive task. The paper also reviews the Multi-Frame Lighting Method [BS96], a proposition to simulate global illumination for realistic animation. The new algorithm is included in the method to extend it for dealing with any kind of dynamic object. As a general improvement of the method, an interpolated-based approach is presented. We apply such approach to obtain motion blur effects of animated sequences.

Keywords: Animation, Dynamic Light Sources, Monte Carlo, Radiosity, Motion Blur

1 Introduction

An important topic of realistic animation is the accurate computation of the illumination of the animated environments. To meet this goal, global illumination models must be considered. However, these models are in general expensive even for a single static scene, therefore, they need to be improved in order to perform efficiently the computation of many frames. The fact that animation changes are smooth between frames, is currently used to develop techniques that exploit coherence in illumination changes. A significant computation time can be saved by reusing global illumination solutions that have been computed in previous frames of the animation.

The radiosity method allows interactive walkthroughs since it is a view-independent global illumination solution. For this reason, it is an appropriate method to be used both in animations and in interactive applications. Many works with a focus on this last domain of applications were proposed. Different strategies like progressive refinements methods [Che90, GSG90, MS94], hierarchical radiosity [FYT94, Sha97, DS97] or image based rendering [NDR96] were developed with the goal of quickly update the changes in illumination for a given demand. In the case of non-interactive animation, however, the needs are not exactly the same as in interactive ones. The illumination of a high number of known frames must be computed with a minimum level of accuracy.

The Multi-Frame Lighting Method proposes an efficient solution for animated radiosity environments by processing many frames of a given animation at once, within a single simulation. The method, based on global Monte Carlo techniques, allows to produce a radiosity representation of a full animation that can be rendered from different animated cameras. The method as it is presented in [BS96] is restricted to static lights sources. Dynamic light sources are in general the most difficult kind of objects to treat because primary energy distribution changes for each frame and therefore less coherence between successive frames can be exploited.

In this paper we present an algorithm to deal with dynamic light sources. The algorithm follows the same philosophy of the Multi-Frame Lighting Method to perform a multi-simulation Monte Carlo shooting-from-lights pass in an efficient way. We also introduce an interpolated-based approach that improve the method by interpolating radiosity solutions in-between full computed ones at key frames. In this way the processing time of the simulation and the memory storage needed decrease. We apply this approach to generate motion blur effects on animated sequences.

Section 2 presents backgrounds of animated radiosity environments and section 3 reviews the Multi-Frame Lighting Method. In section 4 we describe and analyze the new algorithm to deal with dynamic light sources, and section 5 the interpolated based approach. Results obtained are shown in section 6 and conclusions and future work are presented in section 7.

2 Background

Dynamic environments are defined as environments where the number of objects, their shape, location or surface attributes, as reflectance or emittance, may change. Most of previous work on it rely on techniques that update changes in global illumination, for a given modification, at interactive rates. In non-interactive animation, the global illumination problem is more simple because all changes in the environment are known in advance. Nevertheless, a high quality simulation must be performed to improve a realistic sequence.

In [Sha97] an analysis for dynamic environments is presented from a hierarchical radiosity perspective. According to this analysis the links between static surfaces (called environment-environment links in [Sha97]) are the hardest to identify. This is due to the fact that the visibility between any pair of surfaces could be affected by changes in geometry. Drettakis and Sillion, [DS97], used an auxiliary shaft culling structure in their line-space approach to manage this problem. In [Sha97], a motion volume of dynamic objects is built and used in conjunction with a clipping algorithm to quickly detect changes in visibility. The Multi-Frame Lighting Method address the visibility problem through time-independent lines using global Monte Carlo techniques. The method is reviewed in the next section.

3 Review of the Multi-Frame Lighting Method (MFLM)

Global Monte Carlo techniques [Sbe97] have been proposed as an alternative to Monte Carlo radiosity methods. While classic Monte Carlo cast rays from surfaces, global Monte Carlo cast lines that are independent from the surfaces position. These lines are called global lines and one way to build them is to take two random points in a bounding sphere of the whole scene. The fact that these global lines are still valid to compute light energy when surfaces are moved, was used to develop the MFLM.

For a certain animated environment description, first, we record all transformations of dynamic objects at each frame. Then, global lines are cast to compute the light energy exchange between visible surfaces in each frame separately. Dynamic objects are intersected at all instants of time by inversely transforming the lines, this is equivalent to intersect the objects at all position but with the advantage that only one geometry instance of the object is stored. For each global line we obtain a list of objects intersected, each element of the list is labeled with the number of the frame it belongs to. In the following step, independent visibility lists for each frame are built from the list of intersections by separating this list per frames. The multi-path algorithm, described in [SPNP96], is used to compute the lighting exchanges between visible patches.

Figure 1 and 2 illustrates the lighting simulation steps in the MFLM. The simulation can be considered as a global illumination computation of a more complex static scene.

3.1 Efficiency of the method

The cost of the method is studied in [BS96]. An important aspect from the analysis is that the cost processing per frame decreases as the number of frames of the animation grows. This means that the more frames we are processing for a given animated environment the more efficient the method is. We explain here, in an intuitive manner, why it is an efficient method. In a Monte Carlo simulation, light energy is transported through random paths simulated by lines. In our case, when a global line intersects the environment without intersecting the dynamic part of the animation, k different paths, each one for each frame, are updated for the same pairs of intersections. On the other hand, if a global line intersects a dynamic object at many instants, the list of intersections is separated by frames and also k different paths, between the environment and the object or the environment, are updated for the same intersection of the environment. Therefore, the difficult step of identifying visibility changes in environment-environment links is managed in a natural way within the MFLM.

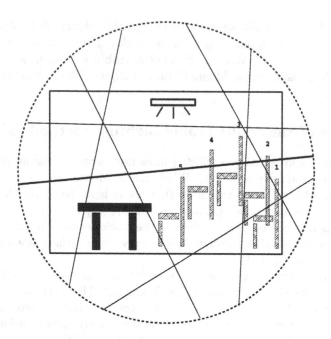

Figure 1: The Multi-Frame lighting Method: Global lines are cast to intersect objects at many instants of time.

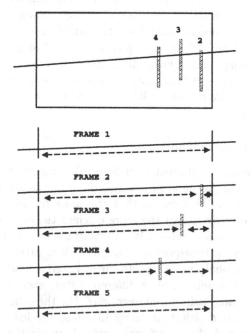

Figure 2: Lists are separated by frames to build independent visibility lists that are used to compute light energy exchanges. In this figure, the thick global line of figure 1 is taken as example.

Although we must intersect all objects at all times, all intersections are useful and no auxiliary visibility structure is needed.

3.2 Animation Processing

Once an animation is completely designed, classic animation softwares acts by transforming all dynamic objects and camera parameters for each frame to compute and stores the resulting render images. A different pipeline is used within the MFLM (see figure 3). The scene environment and the animation description are taken as input for the method. Any animation tool that provides a way to record an animation description could be used. After the lighting simulation is finished, a radiosity representation of the whole animation is stored in a file. This representation is completely view independent, a property of radiosity solutions. This mean that any animated camera description can be used to visualize and obtain the final images of the animation. For this last step we use a hardware graphics z-buffer, which has a relative low cost processing. Thus, many different animations could be obtained with the only cost of this step.

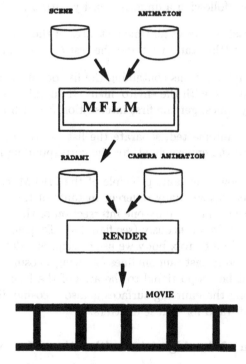

Figure 3: Animation processing in the MFLM. After the lighting simulation, a view independent radiosity representation of the animation (RADANI) is recorded and rendered from an animated camera.

4 An Algorithm for Dynamic Light Sources

Animations where lights sources are in motion are streamly demanding because less illumination coherence can be exploited as a consequence that different distributions of primary energy are required for each frame. As it is exposed in [BS96] the MFLM is restricted to static light sources. This restriction comes from the explicitly first shot step performed by casting lines from light sources. The distribution of primary energy is a necessary step in global Monte Carlo methods because some energy must be carried by global lines in order to perform efficiently the simulation. We present an algorithm to distribute direct light energy from dynamic sources that can be included in the MFLM.

Given an animation description which includes changes in the light sources of the environment and after recording the required transformation to start the MFLM, the algorithm follows this steps:

1. Compute a convex bounding body that encloses the motion of the dynamic source

2. Cast global lines following a uniform density within the body

3. For each line cast, intersect all time instances of the source and the rest of the environment (the static part and the rest of the animation)

4. Build a list of intersections containing the list of source intersections and the first intersection with the environment. If an animated object is intersected at many times, get the first intersection for each frame

5. For each source intersected, separate the list by frames and transfer the power energy to the environment, for the corresponding frame.

The algorithm follows the same principle of the MFLM: cast lines that are useful to transport energy at many different instants of time. In this case the efficiency is seen noting that for only one intersection of the environment many frames can be updated simultaneously (see figure 4). To generate a uniform distribution of lines within a convex body we use a technique described in [Sbe97]: from each face of the body cast random lines following a cosine distribution. The number of lines must be proportional to the area of the face. The distribution of global lines crossing the emitting surfaces is also a cosine distribution, thus, this algorithm is only valid for diffuse emitters.

4.1 Combination of the Algorithm with Other Methods

Although the algorithm described here was conceived for the MFLM, it is independent of it. The algorithm can also be used to distribute direct illumination of a dynamic light source in combination with other illumination methods. Once the primary energy is distributed with the algorithm, the obtained solution could be used to compute the indirect illumination of the animation with any other available illumination method.

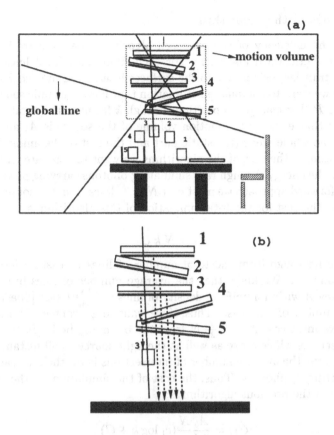

Figure 4: Dynamic Light Sources Algorithm. Global lines are cast from a convex bounding body of the motion volume to transfer direct illumination (a). For each source intersected in the line, transfer power energy to surfaces in the corresponding frame (b)

4.2 Analysis of the algorithm

To analyze the efficiency of the proposed algorithm, we compare it with the following straightforward approach: For each frame cast local lines from the sources and transfer their power to the surfaces intersected in such frames.

Suppose we want to compute an animation that has a dynamic source of area A and power P that changes in position through k frames. The total area of the convex body that encloses the motion volume of the source is A_b and the cost to intersect the whole scene (the static part and the rest of the animation) is C.

Let us estimate the cost of the algorithms we want to compare. If we decide to distribute the energy through rays simulating photons carrying power ϕ, using the straightforward approach we must cast $N = \frac{P}{\phi}$ lines from the source, for each frame. Thus, the cost for the total simulation of this algorithm is:

$$C_I = N \, k \, C \qquad (1)$$

With the new algorithm the total number of lines to cast is derived from Integral Geometry. We know that the average number of lines intersecting a surface of area A within a uniform density of lines is $\frac{2AN_{tot}}{A_b}$ (see [Sbe93]), where N_{tot} is the number of lines cast. Thus, if we want to guarantee N lines crossing the source we must cast $N_{tot} = \frac{A_b}{2A}N$ from the bounding body. In this case, we must intersect the whole scene as well as the light source at all instants of time. Considering that the average number of intersections is n_i, then for each line we are transporting n_i photons. Thus, the cost of the simulation for the same light transport as in the previous algorithm is:

$$C_{II} = \frac{A_b}{2A} \frac{N}{n_i} (c_1 \log k + C) \qquad (2)$$

where c_1 is a constant.

Therefore, our algorithm would be more efficient if the following expression is true:

$$\frac{A_b}{2An_i}(c_1 \log k + C) < kC \qquad (3)$$

Although we are intersecting more surfaces in the proposed algorithm, the cost is reduced by the multiplied factor $\frac{A_b}{2An_i}$. This factor must be always less than k, otherwise the straightforward algorithm is more efficient, and should be used instead. We can say that the algorithm will be more efficient as more emitter surfaces per line are intersected (n_i high), or in other words, that many frames lie in a reduced motion volume. Figure 5 shows three frames of two different animations of light sources: In 5.a the proposed algorithm would be efficient whereas in 5.b the straightforward algorithm would be better.

5 Interpolated-based Improvement

We propose an interpolated-based improvement that can be applied to the new algorithm presented as well as to the MFLM. The fact that illumination changes

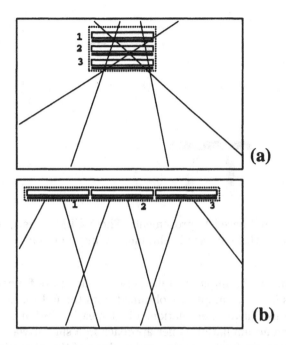

Figure 5: Two light sources animation. In (a) the new algorithm will work efficiently once each global line transport many paths, but in (b) it is better to distribute locally from the sources.

in animations are smooth can be exploited as coherence to improve the MFLM. Nimeroff et al. [NDR96], introduced interpolation of indirect illumination in their framework for animated environment. We propose to interpolate radiosities at object space. The MFLM simulation is performed in the same way as the original proposition but with a lower number of frames. Intermediate radiosity solution frames are obtained by interpolation of full computed (see figure 6). In this way we would improve both time processing and memory required. The cost of processing decreases because less number of objects are intersected and less memory storage is required as only the full computed frames are recorded.

5.1 Motion Blur Effects

Motion blur effects are frequently used in animations with the goal of increasing realism. To keep a realistic simulation of such effect, a physically based lighting method must be improved to compute all light energy interactions between surfaces in the time interval the camera shutter is open. Although several motion blur algorithms have been proposed for different rendering methods, very few consider the computation of all diffuse interreflection in such time interval. In [BP98], an accurate method that solves the illumination equation over time is described. We propose here the use of the interpolated-based approach described above to obtain an approximated solution of the motion blur effect. First, we

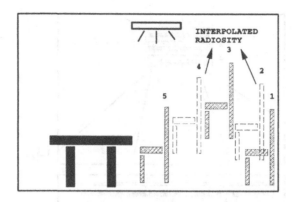

Figure 6: Interpolated-based Improvement. The MFLM is performed for grey objects, radiosity of white objects is obtained by interpolation.

decide on the number of samples to take between successive frames, then interpolated solutions for each sample are obtained from the full solutions computed at the frames, we use linear interpolation. Finally, each solution is projected and combined using an accumulation buffer approach in a similar way as in [HA90]. The whole process is performed in the render phase of the animation processing (see figure 3), that is, after the illumination simulation is finished.

6 Results

To study the efficiency of the dynamic light sources algorithm we compare the two algorithms described in the section 4, We built two different animations in the same environment. In both animation there are dynamic lights and objects, figure 7 and 8 shows some frames of these animations. In the first frame of each animation the motion volume that covers the space of motion of the light is indicated. Both animation are composed by 31 frames.

For the first animation, the average number of intersections inside the motion volume is $n_i = 8.56$, and the factor $\frac{A_b}{2An_i} = 0.45$ and for the second animation, $n_i = 3.97$ and $\frac{A_b}{2An_i} = 2.24$. According to the analysis of section 4.2 this factor must be small to improve the algorithm.

Animation	Algorithm	Direct illumination	Total simulation	Time per frame
First	Straightforward	713	744	24.0
	New	93	124	4.0
Second	Straightforward	719	750	24.2
	New	211	242	7.8

Table 1: Time executions comparisons of the algorithms for the animation of figure 8. All times are measured in minutes.

Table 1 compares time processing between algorithms described in section 4.2. Our algorithm performed 6.0 times faster than the straightforward ap-

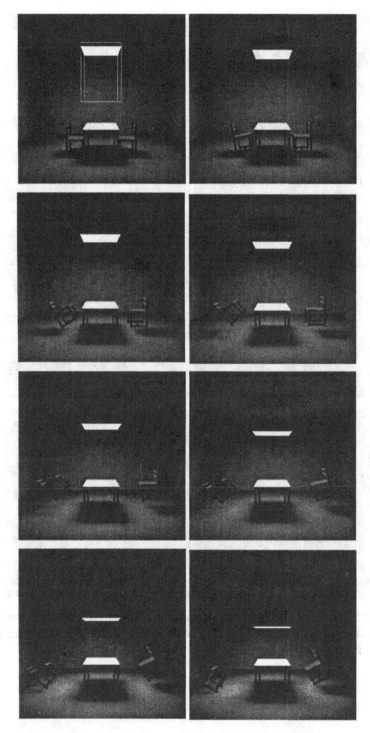

Figure 7: Eight frames of the first animation. Motion volume of the dynamic light is indicated at the first image. The sequence should be read from left to right and from top to bottom.

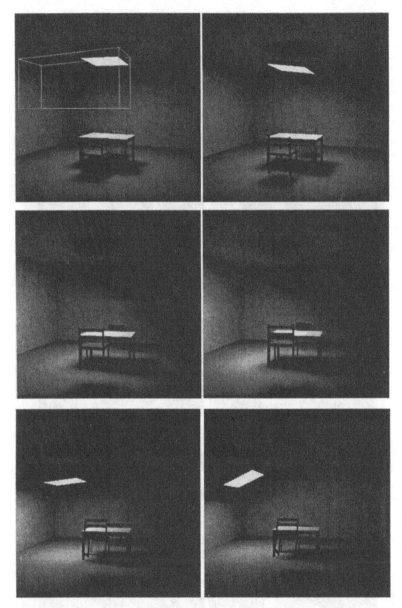

Figure 8: Six frames of the second animation. Motion volume of the dynamic light is indicated at the first image. The sequence should be read from left to right and from top to bottom.

proach for the first animation and 3.1 times for the second one. All executions were measured on a SGI Indigo2 with a R4000 processor. We observe that the efficiency is lower in the second animation because the factor $\frac{A_b}{2An_i}$ is greater. Color images and animations of this results are can be seen at http://ima.udg.es/~gonzalo/images.html.

6.1 Motion Blur

Results of the motion blur method described in 5 are shown in the Apendix. For these images we use 16 samples for each frame. A short animation composed of 10 frames in this environment took about 2 minutes per frame for the illumination computation. Intermediate position and radiosities are interpolated in the rendering step. We project the scene at each sample time and accumulate the resulted images in a frame-buffer. This step took about 30 seconds per frame. Typical details of radiosity scenes, as soft shadows and color bleeding can be observed under the object in motion (see figures 7 and 8).

7 Conclusions and Future Work

We present a new algorithm for dynamic diffuse light sources in radiosity environments. The algorithm is included in the Multi-Frame Lighting Method in order to extend it to deal with all sort of animated objects. From the analysis of the algorithm we conclude that it is an efficient approach for animations when many frames of the dynamic object lie in a reduced motion volume. The algorithm could also be used to distribute direct illumination independently of the MFLM, for example, could be used as a first shoot step and combined with another global illumination methods. We also describe an interpolated-based improvement to the MFLM and we apply it to obtain motion blur effect in animations.

An adaptive strategy to deal with the meshing of the surfaces would improve our method. In general, this is a critical aspect in Monte Carlo algorithms. When dealing with dynamic environments, in addition, variation of the meshing according to the amount of energy of the surfaces exchange may be considered. The combination of our method with hierarchical radiosity approaches could be studied in order to manage the meshing. Our future work include this topic as well as the develop of techniques that exploit temporal coherence for acceleration the intersection process in the our method.

8 Acknowledgment

The authors wish to thank Mateu Sbert and Ignacio Martín for helpful comments. This project has been funded in part with CICYT grant number TIC 95-614-C03-03 and grant 1997SGR00241 of DGR (Generalitat de Catalunya).

References

[BP98]   Gonzalo Besuievsky and Xavier Pueyo. A motion blur method for animated radiosity environments. In Vaclav Skala, editor, *WSCG '98 (Sixth European Conference in Central Europe on Computer Graphics and Visualization)*, pages 35–40, Plzen, Czech Republic, 1998. University of West Bohemia.

[BS96]   Gonzalo Besuievsky and Mateu Sbert. The Multi-Frame Lighting Method: A Monte Carlo Based Solution for Radiosity in Dynamic Environments. *Rendering Techniques '96 (Proceedings of the Seventh Eurographics Workshop on Rendering)*, pages 185–194, 1996.

[Che90] Shenchang Eric Chen. Incremental Radiosity: An Extension of Progressive Radiosity to an Interactive Image Synthesis System. *Computer Graphics (ACM SIGGRAPH '90 Proceedings)*, 24(4):135–144, August 1990.

[DS97]   George Drettakis and Francois X. Sillion. Interactive update of global illumination using a line-space hierarchy. In *Computer Graphics (ACM SIGGRAPH '97 Proceedings)*, volume 31, pages 57–64, 1997.

[FYT94] David A. Forsyth, Chien Yang, and Kim Teo. Efficient Radiosity in Dynamic Environments. In *Fifth Eurographics Workshop on Rendering*, pages 313–323, Darmstadt, Germany, June 1994.

[GSG90] David W. George, Francois X. Sillion, and Donald P. Greenberg. Radiosity Redistribution for Dynamic Environments. *IEEE Computer Graphics and Applications*, 10(4):26–34, July 1990.

[HA90]   P. Haeberky and K. Akeley. The accumultaion buffer. *Computer Graphics (ACM SIGGRAPH '90 Proceedings)*, 23(3):309–318, August 1990.

[MS94]   Stefan Muller and Frank Schoffel. Fast Radiosity Repropagation for Interactive Virtual Environments Using a Shadow-Form-Factor-List. In *Fifth Eurographics Workshop on Rendering*, pages 325–342, Darmstadt, Germany, June 1994.

[NDR96] Jeffry Nimeroff, Julie Dorsey, and Holly Rushmeier. Implementation and analysis of an image-based global illumination fraework for animated environments. *IEEE Transactions on Visualization and Computer Graphics*, 2(4):283–298, December 1996.

[Sbe93] Mateu Sbert. An Integral Geometry Based Method for Fast Form Factor Computation. In *Computer Graphics Forum (Eurographics '93)*, volume 12, pages C409–C420, Barcelona, Spain, September 1993.

[Sbe97] Mateu Sbert. *The Use of Global Random Directions to Compute Radiosity: Global Monte Carlo Techniques*. PhD thesis, Universitat Politecnica de Catalunya, Barcelona, Spain, 1997.

[Sha97] Erin Shaw. Hierarchical radiosity for dynamic environments. *Computer Graphics Forum*, 16(2):107–118, June 1997.

[SPNP96] Mateu Sbert, Xavier Pueyo, Lazlo Neumann, and Werner Purgath-ofer. Global Multipath Monte Carlo Algorithms for Radiosity. *The Visual Computer*, 12(2):47–61, 1996.

From Psychological and Real-Time Interaction Requirements to Behavioural Simulation

Guillaume Moreau,* Stéphane Donikian †

IRISA / SIAMES team

Campus de Beaulieu

F-35042 Rennes, FRANCE

E-mail: gmoreau@irisa.fr, donikian@irisa.fr

Abstract

Behavioural models offer the ability to simulate autonomous entities like organisms and living beings. Psychological studies have showed that the human behaviour can be described by a perception-decision-action loop, in which the decisional process is somehow real-time, concurrent, and hierarchical. Building such systems for interactive simulation requires the design of a reactive system treating flows of data to and from the environment, in a complex way requiring modularity, concurrency and hierarchy, and involving task control and preemption. Accordingly, in this paper we address the adequateness to the decisional part of the behavioural model of Hierarchical Parallel Transition Systems (HPTS). An application consisting in the simulation of a transportation system shows how these HPTS can be of use.

Keywords: Lifelike Behaviours, Interactive Simulation, Reactive Systems.

1 Introduction

The objective of animation is the computation of an image sequence corresponding to discrete time states of an evolving system. Animation consists at first of expressing relationships linking successive states (specification phase) and then making an evaluation of them (execution phase). Motion control models are the heart of any animation/simulation system that determines the friendliness of the user interface, the class of motions and deformations produced, and the application fields. Motion control models can be classified into three general families: descriptive, generative and behavioural models. Descriptive models are used to reproduce an effect without any knowledge about its cause. This kind of models include key frame animation techniques and procedural methods. Unlike the preceding models, generative models offer a causal description of objects movement (describe the cause which produces the effects), for instance, their mechanics. In this case, the user control consists in applying

---

*INRIA
†CNRS

torques and forces to the physical model. Thus, it is not easy to determine causes which can impose some effects onto the mechanical structure to produce a desired motion. Two kinds of tools have been designed for the motion control problem: loosely and tightly coupled control. The loosely coupled control method consists in automatically computing the mechanical system inputs from the last value of the state vector and from the user specification of the desired behaviour, while in the other method, the motion control is achieved by determining constraint equations and by inserting directly these equations into the motion equations of the mechanical system.

Motion control tools provide the user with a set of elementary actions, but it is difficult to control simultaneously a large number of dynamic entities. The solution consists in adding a higher level which controls the set of elementary actions. This requires to make a deliberative choice of the object behaviour, and is done by the third model named *behavioural*. The goal of the behavioural model is to simulate autonomous entities like organisms and living beings [1, 2]. A behavioural entity has the following capabilities: perception of its environment, decision, action and communication [3, 4, 5]. Most behavioural models have been designed for some particular examples in which possible interactions between an object and its environment are very simple: sensors and actuators are reduced to minimal capabilities. Another point which is generally not treated is the notion of time. The issues adressed here are wider; we aim to describe a general formalism of behaviour modeling based on psychological studies and compatible with real-time constraints.

In this paper, we will start by analyzing the decisional architectures defined by behavioural psychologists and which may be compatible with real-time. Then we will make a short review of the techniques employed in the realm of behavioural animation. After discussing the pros and cons of known approaches, we will introduce the HPTS formalism and show its usefulness thanks to a behaviour description language. An autonomous car driver model is then presented: it is applied to the realm of virtual urban environments and automated highways (through the DIATS project).

2 Psychological requirements

According to Newell [6], the constraints of a computer behavioural model are the following:

- adaptative and flexible behaviour,
- real-time interaction with the environment,
- complex and rich environment, i.e., a behavioural entity should be able to perceive its environment, should have a knowledge database and several degrees of freedom of actions on the environment.
- use of symbols and abstraction,
- ability to learn,
- autonomy in a social background (ie. possible social interactions with other entities),
- self-consciousness and perception,

- realizable as a neural network, constructable by an embryological growth process, and arise through evolution.

Of course, the three last constraints expressed in the last item will not be adressed in this paper. In fact we essentially focus on the three first constraints, because considering the level reached by computer science today, it is not possible yet to deal with symbolic reasoning in real-time. Therefore, our goal is to build a model which will allow some adaptative and flexible behaviour to any entity evolving in a complex environment and interacting with other entities. Interactive execution is also fundamental.

Mallot [7], among others, describes the interactions between a behavioural entity and its environment (see in figure 1). The overview of the system is a perception-decision-action loop. The first arrow from sensors to actuators is called homeostasy (ie. the internal regulation feedback) whereas the second arrow stands for the actions required for perception (e.g. turning the head to see something which should be on the left).

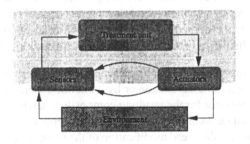

Figure 1: The human organism and its environment.

Lord [8] introduces several paradigms about the way the brain works and controls the remainder of the human body. He explains that human behaviour is naturally hier-archical, that cognitive functions of the brain are run in parallel. Moreover cognitive functions are different in nature: some are purely reactive, while other require more time. Executions times and frequencies of the different activities are provided. This has lead us to state that paradigms required for programming a *realistic* behavioural model are:

- reactivity, which encompasses sporadic or asynchronous events and exceptions,
- modularity in the behaviour description, which allows parallelism and concur-rency of sub-behaviours,
- data-flow, for the specification of the communication between different modules,

- hierarchical structuring of the behaviour, which means the possibility of preempt-ing sub-behaviours on transitions in the meta-behaviour, as a kind of exception or interruption. It means also that sub-behaviours can notify the meta-behaviour of their activity.
- frequency handling for execution of sub-behaviours. This provides the ability to model reaction times in perception activities.

3 Behavioural animation: state of the art

3.1 First generation of behavioural systems

Different approaches have been studied for the decision part of behavioural models:

Sensor-effector Approach. The behaviour of objects is defined by sensors, effectors and a network of intermediate nodes (neural networks for example) which connects them. The way an object behaves in the environment depends on how the environment is sensed, and how this information is passed through the network to the effectors that produce the motion of the object. The same neural network can produce different kinds of motion depending on the parameterization of nodes and on the weight of connections (see e.g. [9]).

Behaviour Rule Approach. Like the previous approach, it takes sensed information as its input and motor controls as its output, but the behaviour of the object is controlled by a set of behaviour rules. The possible behaviours can be represented by a decision tree in which each branch represents one alternative behaviour (see e.g. [10]). This method offers a higher level of description than the preceding one, but the difficulty results from the choice of the rating strategy.

Finite Automaton Approach. In this approach, the behaviour of an object is either controlled by one finite automaton or by combining elementary behaviours and designing a supervisor for the resulting composite behaviour. The use of a single automaton is not convenient: firstly making conceptually simple changes in behaviours requires widespread modification of the finite state machine, secondly it is difficult to express concurrent constraints on control processes [11].

Most of these systems have been designed for some particular examples, in which modularity and concurrency are not necessary. Behavioural entities have only one activity line and because interactions between an object and its environment are very simple: sensors and actuators are reduced to minimal capabilities which, most of the time, only allow to obstacle avoidance in a 2D or 3D world. Another point which is generally not treated is the notion of time, while it is necessary, either during the specification phase (memorisation, prediction, action duration) or during the execution phase (synchronisation of objects with different internal times).

3.2 Second generation: state machines based systems

More recently, a second generation of behavioural models has been developed to describe the human behaviour in specific tasks. As human behaviour is very complex, none of the preceding models could be applied. The common characteristics of these new models are: reactivity, parallelism and different abstract levels of behaviours. In [12], a tennis game application is shown, including the behaviour of players and referees. A stack of automata is used to describe the behaviour of each actor. It is possible to decompose a complex behaviour in sub-behaviours by using this stack: one automaton can push itself with the current state on the stack and switch to the new automaton which is able to reach the specific sub-goal. As humans are deliberative agents, purely reactive systems are not sufficient to describe their behaviour. It is necessary to integrate both cognitive and reactive aspects of behaviour. Cognitive models are rather motivated by the representation of the agent's knowledge (beliefs and intentions). Intentions enable an agent to reason about its internal state and that of others. The centre of such a deliberative agent is its own representation of the world which includes a representation of the mental state of itself and of other agents with which he is currently interacting. To do this, Badler et al. [13] propose to combine Sense-Control-Action (SCA) loops with planners and PaT-Nets. SCA loops define the reflexive behaviour and are continuous systems which interconnect sensors and effectors through a network of nodes, exactly like in the sensor effector approach described above. PaT-Nets are essentially finite state automata that can be executed in parallel (for example the control of the four fingers and of the thumb for a grasping task). The planner queries the state of the database through a filtered perception to decide how to elaborate the plan and to select an action. In all these systems, the action is directly associated with each node, which doesn't allow the management of concurrency.

From our point of view [3], different paradigms are required to describe a deliberative behavioural model: we have to design a *reactive system* continuously in communication with its environment (*data-flow*). The behaviour of a creature, even for the simplest, is composed of different activity lines (*modularity*) which can be completely distinct but also *concurrent*. *Hierarchy* and *preemption* are some other important notions for such a system, because they enable users to build it in a modular and re-usable way, defining behaviours from sub-behaviours, sequenced, interrupted or suspended by preemption. Kearney et al. [14] have proposed to use Hierarchical Concurrent State Machines (HCSM): a state machine may contain multiple, concurrently executing sub-state machines. A state-machine has a control panel consisting of buttons and dials that provides a communication interface between the state machine and the world outside it. Each active state machine outputs one or several values determined by the activity associated function. The values output by the top level HCSM are used as inputs for the entity to control. We proposed to use a Hierarchy of Parallel Transition Systems (HPTS), which can be viewed as an extension of HCSM which defines more precisely the message passing through the hierarchy of transition systems or state machines. Another important extension is that HPTS manage temporal aspects (delay, minimal and maximal durations, frequency) of Transition Systems, which are very important for the behaviour realism. In the remainder of this paper, we will first present our behavioural model based on Hierarchical Parallel Transition Systems (HPTS) and then illustrate its implementation for a complex human task: drive a vehicle.

4 A Model for Behavioural Animation

4.1 Hierarchical Parallel Transition Systems

The Decisional model consists of a reactive system, which is composed of a hierarchy of state machines (possible behaviours). Each state machine of the system can be viewed as a black-box with an In/Out data-flow and a set of control parameters. It can be defined by the following tuple $< S, \Gamma, IS, OS, CP, LV, IF, MB >$ in which:

S : is a set of sub-state machines,   **CP** : is a set of Control Parameters,
Γ : is the activity function,   **LV** : is a set of Local Variables,
IS : is a set of Input Signals,   **IF** : is the integration function,
OS : is a set of Output Signals,   **MB** : is a Mail-Box.

State Machine.   Each state machine of the system is either an atomic state machine
($S = \emptyset$), or a composite state machine. An activity parameter is associated to each state
machine which corresponds to the current status of this machine. This parameter is
accessible by using the function *status(state, instant)*, which has three possible value:

$$(\forall s \in S)(\forall k \in \mathcal{N}), \, status(s, t_k) \in \{active, idle, wait\}$$

There is also an optional duration parameter which is used to force the state machine to
keep a state active for a minimum duration. This allows the modelling of reaction times.
On the contrary, the maximum duration of the active phase can also be specified. When
this value is reached, an event is generated in order to warn the system that something
that should have happened actually did not.

The status of a state machine is described by an automaton (cf figure 2), in which
transitions between the three status depend on events produced either by the meta-state
(preemption) or by the state itself (auto-termination). A specific method is attached to
each transition (start, suspend, resume and terminate the task) and also to the active
status (execute).

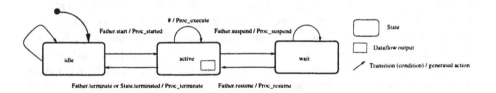

Figure 2: Status Management Automaton.

The activity function.   Activity of a state evolves during the simulation, and this is
determined by an activity function Γ. This function has four parameters and returns the
new status:

$$(\forall s \in S)(\forall k \in \mathcal{N}^*), \, status(s, t_k) = \Gamma(status(s, t_{k-1}), IS, CP, LV)$$

This function permits to represent some transitions between different sub-state machines, but more than one sub-state can be active at each instant (concurrency). This
function handles also hierarchical preemption, by the fact that one argument of the function is a set of Control Parameters (CP) which allows to deal with internal events such
as "sub-state *i* is *terminated*" or external events such as "*the traffic lights become red*".

Input / Output parameters.   Input and output parameters are continuous signals of
standard type (e.g. integer, real, boolean for example). The value of an Output signal is

undetermined when the state machine is *idle* or *suspended*. Outputs are used to return actions proposed by the state-machine.

Local variables. Local variables are some variables of standard type, whose value is computed by using the Ω function. Local variables can either retain their values between activations or be reinitialized on each reactivation (*started* status):

$$(\forall v \in V)(\forall k \in \mathcal{N}^*), \; value(v, t_k) = \Omega(value(v, t_{k-1}), status(s, t_{k-1}), IS, CP)$$

Control parameters. Control parameters allow to modulate the behaviour of an entity, depending on external or internal decision. The type of a control parameter is either boolean or interval (*value* $\in [Vmin, Vmax]$). For example, a sub-process can inform its parent process that its specific task has been achieved and that its status becomes *terminated*, while a process can notify another sub-process that it has to be *started*.

The integration function. The integration function has to manage the coherence of the actions proposed by the different sub-processes, and make a synthesis of them. This is in fact a function which takes as inputs the outputs of all sub-processes and delivers the value of the process outputs. In the case of concurrent behaviours proposed by different sub-state machines, this function has to make a choice and to deliver a unified behaviour as output of the state machine (cf figure 3).

$$OS = IF(output(S), LV, CP)$$

The Mail-Box The Mail-Box is used to manage communication between state-machines. A message can be sent to a specific list of state-machines, sent to state-machines which have expressed (by subscribing) their interest to this kind of message or broadcasted to all state-machines.

Example An example of a state machine is given in figure 3. The state machine *Supervisor* is a state-machine that includes three concurrent state-machines (*SM1*, *SM2* and *SM3*). These state-machines are purely sequential and the activity function may be represented by transitions. On the right, the data-flows associated with the state-machine are represented; the integration function shows here that the a output of *Supervisor* is the average of the a output of *SM1* and the b output of *SM2*.

4.2 Behaviour description language

Our model of a behavioural entity is based on the HPTS formalism, i.e. Hierarchical Parallel Transition Systems and data-flows. Though they may be coded directly with an imperative programming language like C++, we decided to build a language for behaviour description. Otherwise the problem is that it quickly becomes quite difficult to update a complex state machine and therefore to reuse it in future developments. Moreover the code of the transition systems becomes unreadable or inefficient. This is why we propose a language that allows the description of both the hierarchical parallel state machines and their associated data-flows. This language is compiled and efficient C++ code is generated. The change of a transition condition is thus quite easy.

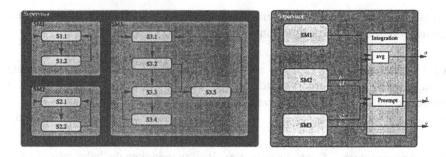

Figure 3: State-Transition and data-flow aspects of the state machine.

4.2.1 Architecture of the language

Our language fully implements the HTPS formalism. The goal is the (object-oriented) design of behavioural entities, at least for their reactive part, and the connection with tasks that require more computation time. In this section we will provide a short description of the grammar (in a BNF-like form) of our language. Keywords are written in bold, whereas italic typeface represents a non-terminal rule. A * stands for a 0..n repetition while a + stands for a 1..n repetition. | is the alternative operator and a statement enclosed in {} is optional.

The description of a state machine is done in the following way: the body of the declaration contains a list of states and a list of transitions between these states.

smachine	::=	**SMACHINE** *Id* { *sm-definition* }
sm-definition	::=	*initial-state* {*state*}+ {*transition*}+
initial-state	::=	**INITIAL** *Id* ;
state	::=	*Id* { *duration* } ; { *outputs* }
duration	::=	[*float* { *maxd* }]
maxd	::	, *float* , *event*

A state is defined by its name and its activity with regard to data-flows (the *outputs* rule of the grammar is in fact a subset of the C++ language which would be too long to describe). A state accepts an optional duration parameter which stands for the minimum and maximum amount of time spent in the state. A transition is defined by an origin, an extremity and a transition expression. The transition expression consists of two parts: a read-expression which includes the conditions to be fulfilled in order to fire the transition, and a write-expression which is a list of the generated events and basic activity primitives on the state machines.

transition	::=	**TRANSITION** *Id* { *transition-decl* }
transition-decl	::=	*origin-decl extremity-decl expr-evt*
origin-decl	::=	**ORIGIN** *Id* ;
extremity-decl	::=	**EXTREMITY** *Id* ;
expr-evt	::=	*expr-read* {, *expr-read*}* / *expr-write* {, *expr-write*}* ;
expr-read	::=	#	*evt-name*	*sm-read*	*timer-read*	*expr-math*

expr-write	::=	**#** | *evt-name* | *sm-write* | *timer-write*
sm-read	::=	**SMACHINE(** *sm-read-prim* , *sm-name* **)**
sm-read-prim	::=	**end**
sm-write	::=	**SMACHINE(** *sm-write-prim* , *sm-name* **)**
sm-write-prim	::=	**start** | **suspend** | **resume** | **terminate**
timer-read	::=	**TIMER(** *timer-name* **)**
timer-write	::=	**TIMER(** *timer-action* , *timer-name* **)**
timer-action	::=	**start** , *duration*
		| **kill**

There are three different kinds of expressions: the simplest expression is an event expression (*evt-name*) which is in fact the name of the event awaited or generated. The state machine primitives (*sm-write*) stand for the activity functions of the HPTS model. The *sm-read* expression allows a state to wait for the termination of a sub-state. The *timer* primitives provide a basic handling of time through timers which can be set, deleted or waited for. At last, the *expr-math* rule allows to wait for logical combinations of numerical conditions.

4.2.2 Code generation

Once the behavioural entities are described, the parser builds a state machine tree and performs some rewriting operations on it: for instance, a state s which has a minimum duration d is transformed into a couple of states (s_1, s_2) with the same actions; but state s_1 can only be followed by state s_2 after having waited for d seconds, whereas the transitions coming from state s are now coming from state s_2. The same kind of rewriting operations is performed for maximum durations.

Afterwards, C++ code for our simulation platform GASP [15] is generated. It is totally encapsulated: all transitions systems are included in their own class directly inheriting from an abstract state machine class which provides pure virtual methods for running the state machines and debugging methods (display of current state, transitions fired, value of the variables). The advantage of using the object model is that the behaviour simulation code is easy to use in any application. The emphasis in the code generation phase is put on efficiency and connectivity to existing C++ code.

4.2.3 Visual behaviour description language

Despite the benefits of the language approach described earlier, the description of behaviour remains quite difficult to people who are not computer scientists. Therefore we are building a graphical tool which is associated to our behaviour description language, in order to allow behavioural specialists to test their models into an interactive simulation. This project is currently underway and is more than a simple graphical tool for drawing state machines, it also includes a graphical description of the dataflows and the associated integration functions.

5 Driving Simulation

5.1 Environment model for autonomous entities

Each creature must build a mental model of its environment, even for the simplest behaviour. It is necessary to reconstruct the new state of the world, at each simulation step, before using it in the decisional part of the agent. Since it is not possible to update in real time a complete mental model only from vision and image processing, we have to add higher levels of information than the geometrical one in the model of the environment.

Information needed to describe the behaviour of an entity, depends on the nature of this entity, but globally we can decompose it into three kinds : geometric, topologic and semantic levels. The simplest behaviour consists in avoiding static and dynamic obstacles, and this requires only geometrical information on objects in the scene. The behaviour of an entity depends on the nature of objects in its environment. We have to build a semantic level of the scene, which consists in classifying objects at different abstraction levels. Another important aspect is the tactical one: what is the best motion to go from an initial location to a final one, depending on the nature of the motion and on characteristics of the environment? This is performed by adding topological information on the scene.

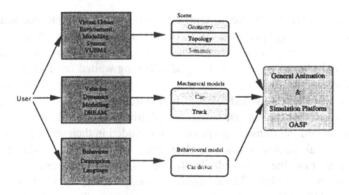

Figure 4: Overall view of the SIAMES Simulation Environment.

In the driving simulation context, we are particularly interested by reproducing the life in the streets, including the interaction of the different transportation systems. The information required is of different kinds: the road network, with its geometry (road-shape), its rules (road-signs) and its environment (buildings, parks, ...). This is enough for driving simulation in which vehicles are all driven by a user in the loop. When autonomous vehicles are added to the simulation, other kinds of information become necessary : qualitative information on the road (straight line, curve), city information (name of streets, neighbourhoods, particular buildings, squares) and topological information on the road network. The SIAMES team at IRISA has therefore developed a complete simulation environment devoted to multimodal traffic simulation, which is based on GASP, our General Animation and Simulation Platform. VUEMS (Virtual Urban Environment Modelling System) [16] enables to build a virtual copy of thoroughfares of real cities. The Modelling System uses, as inputs, different kinds of information: cartographic databases, scanned maps of roadways, traffic lights organisation and working. After the interactive description of the road-network, VUEMS produces two complementary outputs: the 3D geometric representation of the scene (including automatic texturing) and its symbolic representation (geometric, topologic and semantic levels) used by sensors and deliberative agents. The overall architecture of our simulation environment is presented in figure 4.

5.2 Automated car driver

In this section we will describe the automated car driver models that have been implemented whithin GASP (for urban environments and highway driving). We will successively discuss the three components of the "Perception-Decision-Action" model. The global architecture of the system is presented in figure 5. It shows the different modules used in the simulation and the data flows between them. The little filled circle stands for a delay operator; as there are data dependencies between the modules, delays are required to avoid deadlocks; for instance at t, the motion controller gives a torque $\Gamma(t)$ to the dynamic model. The dynamic model uses if to produce $x(t)$ the position of the vehicle center of gravity. But the controller needs some knowledge about the position of the car to compute $\Gamma(t)$. As $x(t)$ is not available yet, the controller must use $x(t - dt)$.

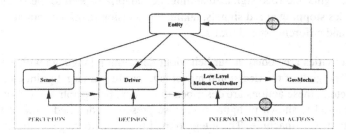

Figure 5: Architecture of the virtual vehicle.

5.2.1 Sensors and perception

In the realm of real-time animation or simulation, it is impossible to completely simulate human vision and the building of a mental model of the environment. Therefore, the automatic driver gets a local view of its environment through a sensor which is in fact a filter of the whole environment database. Two different types of objects are taken into account in the sensor: static objects (buildings, road signals, traffic lights) and dynamic objects (cars, trucks, bicycles). These objects are included as a bounding box in a dynamic grid updated every time step.

Our sensor has two parameters, r its range and α its angle of view. It is localised by a position and an orientation. At each time step, the sensor determines the elements of the grid that belong the vision cone. It then performs a Z-Buffer algorithm on the bounding boxes of the objects, in order to eliminate objects that would be hidden by closer objects. The outputs of the sensor are lists of signals (distance and type) and dynamic objects.

In order not to take into account the behaviour of every vehicle of the environment, the perception model filters the datas issued from the sensor and ignores vehicles which are not in the same road section (or not in its neighbours). Perception then focuses on the eight immediately surrounding vehicules. Only the closest vehicle is taken into account for each zone. Vehicles that have undertaken a lane-change manœuvre belong to two different zones: the zone matching their actual position and the zone towards which they are heading. The same strategy is used with road signals and traffic lights; only the closest signals of the same category are taken into account.

5.2.2 Decisional model

In our model, the car driver performs simultaneously different activities:

- dynamic objects handling, i.e. following the other cars, possibly overtaking them, avoiding pedestrians and cyclists. This matches two concurrent activities due to the speed difference between cars and pedestrians.
- road network following, i.e. following the road, changing lane, taking turns in crossroads. Directions followed in crossroads are at the moment defined statically before the beginning of the simulation.
- traffic lights and road signals handling, i.e. adapting speed to the situation. This includes stopping at red signals, taking the decision to stop or not at orange signals, and enforcing speed limits.

These activities are coded in our behaviour description language with several state machines. The goal of the decisional model is to produce a target point and an action with parameters; these actions are described in the next paragraph. An overview of the decisional model is shown in figure 6. It also presents a detailed view of the traffic lights handling state-machine. The integration of the behaviours generated by the sub-states (the activities performed in parallel) is done as seen previously in figure 3. In fact, there is a preemption on the low-level actions (see 5.2.3) of the motion controller; it is obvious that an emergency stop has a higher priority than a normal drive action. When two sub-behaviours return the same action, a conservative law is applied to the values: the desired speed is the minimum of all desired speeds and the braking distance is the minimum braking distance.

5.2.3 Mechanics of the car and control

As the decisional model is not able by itself to specify guidance and pedal pressure torques, we have added a low-level motion controller providing several parametrized actions which are the actual outputs of the decisional model. These actions are:

- DRIVE(desired speed), the normal mode for driving alone.
- FOLLOW(headway, desired speed), the mode for following the preceding vehicle with the specified headway without either driving faster than the desired speed.

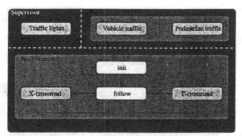 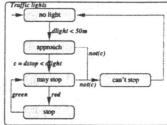

Figure 6: Architecture of the decisional model of an automated car driver in a urban environement and detailed view of the traffic light handling state-machine

- STOP(distance), the mode for stopping the car with the help of the brakes. The DRIVE mode only makes use of engine brake which makes it less efficient.
- EMERGENCY_BRAKE(), namely the mode for stopping the car as soon as possible.

The goal of the low-level controller is to produce a guidance torque, an engine torque and a brake pedal pressure as inputs for the mechanical model. The mechanical aspect of the car is modelled with DREAM [17] our rigid and deformable bodies modeling systems. The effects taken into account in the car model are aerodynamic aspects, inertia of the body and the suspension system. By means of Lagrange's equations, DREAM computes exact motion equations in a symbolic form for analysis and then generates numerical C++ simulation code for GASP.

5.3 Virtual urban environments applications

By now, driving simulations are commonly limited to cars and trucks interactions on highways. Urban traffic has a higher degree of complexity, as it requires interactions on the same thoroughfare between not only cars, trucks, bicyclists and pedestrians, but also public transportation systems as busses and trams. As our approach is modular, we have started to integrate all these transportation modes into GASP, our simulation platform. Mechanical models of trucks and cars are available, as well as kinematic models of bicyclists and pedestrians. We have also recently integrated a model of tram to perform some simulations on a real case study (Croix Bonneaux Crossroads in the city of Nantes). This crossroads is in fact a round-about which is crossed by two tramway tracks which merge inside the crossroads (cf figure 7). Each crossing between a tramway and a roadway is handled by three traffic lights which are controlled by eight sensors on the railway track. These sensors detect when a tram is passing over their specific location and are used to regulate the traffic of vehicles and to give the priority to the tram. We have been asked to study this crossroads to evaluate possibilities of deadlocks due to a high traffic demand. Behavioural models of a car and tram drivers, as well as a biker have been described, and we are still working on the behaviour of the pedestrian which is more complicated as he is not constrained to stay on the thoroughfare but, unlike the others, he can walk everywhere in the city.

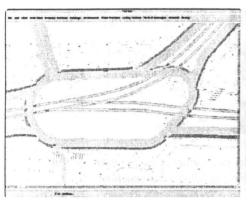

Figure 7: Virtual urban environment modelling and simulation

5.4 The DIATS project

DIATS is a research project sponsored by the European Community. It aims at defining and studying some ATT (Advanced Transport Telematics) scenarios on interurban motorways. As a matter of fact the problems of congestion arising from an increasing number of vehicles on the roads have focused Government Policies towards a more efficient management of the existing road network. ATT systems include AID (Automatic Incident Detection), variable speed limits, ramp metering, AICC (Autonomous Intelligent Cruise Control). The AICC system is a speed controller that takes into account not only the desired speed but also the distance between a car and the preceding vehicle thanks to on-board sensors. Figure 8 presents snapshots of a simulation of vehicles with and without the AICC system. As the AICC reacts really quicker than the "human driver", vehicles on the left are forced to brake when the others can simply rely on engine braking.

The SIAMES team has defined a complete model (sub-microscopic) of a highway driver (architecture in figure 5). Other partners of the DIATS project (TRG, TRL, TUHH) design macroscopic models of the vehicles to study global effects of the ATT systems. In France, INRETS defines a driver model entirely based on psychological and statistical studies. Common measuring parameters have been defined in order to cross-validate simulation results obtained by the different partners of the project.

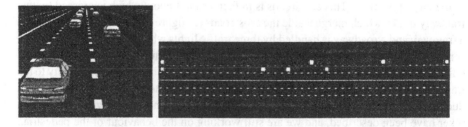

Figure 8: Visualization of the effects of AICC: vehicles on the right lane are equipped, others are not.

6 Conclusion

We have presented in this paper the behavioural model, and more precisely the decisional part of this model. A formal model of a Hierarchical Parallel Transition System has been presented to describe *realistic* behaviours, which requires different programming paradigms: reactivity, concurrency, data-flow and hierarchical preemption. Then we have presented how this formal model has been implemented in a description language which is able to generate efficient C++ code for GASP, our Simulation Platform. The use of Hierarchical Parallel Transition Systems allows us to take into account several programming paradigms important to describe *realistic* behaviours. Because of the integration of our behavioural model in a simulation platform, we have also the ability to deal with real time during the specification and the execution phases.

Our main objective is real-time simulations of several entities evolving in a topographically realistic environment. Many studies have been performed by psychologists to analyse the human behaviour during the driving task, but very few of them have focused their work on pedestrians and bicyclists for example. In order to analyse their behaviour, we decided to make some experiments on real sites and others with walkers and bikers immersion in the corresponding virtual environment. The behavioural model will allow us to describe, in a same way, different kinds of living beings, and to simulate them in the same virtual environment, while most of behavioural models are presently restricted to the animation of one model in a specific environment. Another important point is that our behavioural model has been built to generate dynamic entities which are both autonomous and controllable, allowing us to use the same model in different contexts and moreover with different levels of control.

References

1. N. I. Badler, C. B. Phillips, and B. L. Webber. *Simulating Humans : Computer Graphics Animation and Control.* Oxford University Press, 1993.

2. Norman I. Badler, Bonnie L. Webber, Jugal Kalita, and Jeffrey Esakov, editors. *Making them move: mechanics, control, and animation of articulated figures.* Morgan Kaufmann, 1991.

3. S. Donikian and E. Rutten. Reactivity, concurrency, data-flow and hierarchical preemption for behavioural animation. In E.H. Blake R.C. Veltkamp, editor, *Programming Paradigms in Graphics'95*, Eurographics Collection. Springer-Verlag, 1995.

4. B.M. Blumberg and T.A. Galyean. Multi-level direction of autonomous creatures for real-time virtual environments. In *Siggraph*, pages 47–54, Los Angeles, California, U.S.A., August 1995. ACM.

5. O. Ahmad, J. Cremer, S. Hansen, J. Kearney, and P. Willemsen. Hierarchical, concurrent state machines for behavior modeling and scenario control. In *Conference on AI, Planning, and Simulation in High Autonomy Systems*, Gainesville, Florida, USA, 1994.

6. Allen Newell. *Unified Theories of Cognition.* Harvard University Press, 1990.

7. Hanspeter A. Mallot. Behavior-oriented approaches to cognition : theoretical perspectives. *Theory in biosciences*, 116:196–220, 1997.

8. R. G. Lord and P. E. Levy. Moving from cognition to action : A control theory perspective. *Applied Psychology : an international review*, 43 (3):335–398, 1994.

9. Michiel van de Panne and Eugene Fiume. Sensor-actuator networks. In James T. Kajiya, editor, *Computer Graphics (SIGGRAPH '93 Proceedings)*, volume 27, pages 335–342, August 1993.

10. Xiaoyuan Tu and Demetri Terzopoulos. Artificial fishes: Physics, locomotion, perception, behavior. In *Computer Graphics (SIGGRAPH'94 Proceedings)*, pages 43–50, Orlando, Florida, July 1994.

11. M. Booth, J. Cremer, and J. Kearney. Scenario control for real-time driving simulation. In *Fourth Eurographics Workshop on Animation and Simulation*, pages 103–119, Politechnical University of Catalonia, September 1993.

12. H. Noser and D. Thalmann. Sensor based synthetic actors in a tennis game simulation. In *Computer Graphics International'97*, pages 189–198, Hasselt, Belgium, June 1997. IEEE Computer Society Press.

13. Norman I. Badler, Barry D. Reich, and Bonnie L. Webber. Towards personalities for animated agents with reactive and planning behaviors. *Lecture Notes in Artificial Intelligence, Creating Personalities for synthetic actors*, (1195):43–57, 1997.

14. J. Kearney, J. Cremer, and S. Hansen. Motion control through communicating, hierarchical state machines. In G. Hegron and O. Fahlander, editors, *Fifth Eurographics Workshop on Animation and Simulation*, Oslo, Norway, September 1994.

15. Stéphane Donikian, Alain Chauffaut, Thierry Duval, and Richard Kulpa. Gasp: from modular programming to distributed execution. In *Computer Animation'98*, Philadelphia, USA, June 1998. IEEE Computer Society Press.

16. S. Donikian. Vuems: a virtual urban environment modeling system. In *Computer Graphics International'97*, Hasselt-Diepenbeek, Belgium, June 1997. IEEE Computer Society Press.

17. Rémi Cozot. From multibody systems modelling to distributed real-time simulation. In ACM, editor, *American Simulation Symposium*, New Orleans, USA, 1996.

Identification of Motion Models for Living Beings

Nicolas Pazat and Jean-Luc Nougaret

IRISA, INRIA-RENNES

Campus Universitaire de Beaulieu, 35042 Rennes Cedex, France.

Abstract

Recent trends in computer graphics animation have shown the emergence of two alternative paths towards the quest for realistic motion control. On the one hand, physics-based modeling provides a comprehensive framework to design dynamic motions that can react and adapt to varying environments. On the other hand, advances in motion capture technology have proved to be a practical fast track towards realism. At the beginning of this paper, it will be recalled that none of these approaches is a panacea. In order to mix their respective advantages, the paradigm of motion identification is investigated and illustrated on a study case. Motion identification bridges the gap between dynamic models and motion capture by automatically finding the best match between the possible dynamic behaviors of a specified class of semi-physical models and real-world trajectories. This paper builds upon a vast theoretical tool-box coming from classic Identification theory and discusses how this framework can be applied within the context of animating synthetic living beings. A major point is to show that motion identification requires a radically new way of thinking about dynamic motion models.

Key-words : identification, motion control, dynamic systems, animation

Animation : ftp://ftp.irisa.fr/local/siames/motion/IdentiFish.html

1   Introduction : The Quest for Realism

Although realism is not always necessary in computer graphics animation, controlling the motion of living beings that look natural remains a challenge. First, it must be acknowledged that skilled animators are able to produce convincing motions using widespread tools such as key-framing and inverse kinematics. As an alternative to this work-intensive approach, researchers in computer graphics animation are investigating new tools by which realism can be achieved more automatically. The task is especially difficult when one tries to take additional requirements into account, such as the computational cost or the capability to perform real-time reactive behaviors in presence of varying environments. These features are particularly important for interactive animation as in virtual reality and video-games applications. For the purpose of our discussion, we shall notice that one can roughly distinguish two alternative approaches towards the quest for realism : physics-based modeling and motion capture.

1.1 Physics-based modeling

This approach attempts to achieve realistic motion by simulating (within the virtual world) all the physical laws and phenomenons which apply in the real world. This approach works well (as long as the computational cost can be sustained by the available processor) for *inert* bodies, i.e. for bodies whose motion complies with pure mechanics.

Physics-based modeling suffers severe limitations when dealing with living beings. Indeed, above the skeletal system, the neuro-muscular still largely defies human science. Additionally, modeling its dynamic behavior is particulary intricate. Just to point-out the complexity of modeling living organisms, it is worth noting that natural neuro-muscular control usually outperforms the control systems designed for man-made machines. In other words, the difficulty with living beings arises from the fact that even if one could come out with a detailed mathematical model of natural motion dynamics, its closed-form expression would certainly be extremely complicated up to the point of making it intractible. In the absence of accurate and well-behaved models of natural motion, the control laws must be "guessed" or "hand-crafted" [HBWO95], if not learned from scratch by automated search algorithms, optimizations and heuristics [Coh92, NM93, vdPF93, vdP96, GT95].

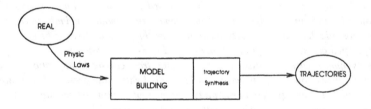

Figure 1: *Physics-based modeling.*

Nevertheless, dynamic models still raise up considerable interest because they possess unequaled capabilities : with dynamic models, trajectories are issued from the simulation, which makes it possible to perform reactive behaviors and to adapt to evolving environments.

1.2 Motion capture technology

Fueled by continuing advances in magnetic and infrared sensor technologies, motion capture has proved to be a practical fast track towards realism. This is not a surprise. Indeed, given the intrinsic complexity and the variety of living systems, it is very tempting to film or acquire real motions and store them for subsequent reuse. But the problem lies at this point : motion reuse. In the literature, this problem has been addressed for different cases in which elementary motions would need to be reused. For instance, one

may wish to apply motion captured trajectories on a synthetic creature with a different skeleton or topology [MBT96, BRRP97].

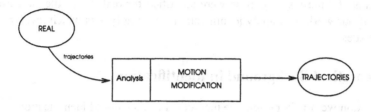

Figure 2: *Motion capture.*

Also, one may want to obtain new motions through the means of computing new transitions, warping and blending from previously captured motions [KB93, UAT95, BW95, RGBC96, GR96]. However, a severe limitation of reusing trajectories obtained with motion capture comes from the fact that the original motion must only undergo minor modifications, otherwise the realism of the trajectory may be lost.

1.3 Going beyond motion capture with dynamic models

As it is usually the case for most classifications, the two above mentioned categories should not be considered as having hermetic borders. Indeed, although several research papers on realistic motion control are more or less clearly tainted as "physics-based" or "motion capture-based", many researchers in the computer graphics community have long perceived the need to cross the borders between these two approaches (for instance see [KB96, HBWO95, Hod96, NAHR95]).

From the above discussion, it can be seen that motion capture on the one hand and physics-based dynamic models on the other hand, feature symmetric pros and cons. Indeed, dynamic models offer uncomparable flexibility in terms of motion production whereas motion capture is the ultimate guarantee in terms of realism. In order to combine the respective advantages of physics-based models and motion capture, the framework of *identification* provides a systematic design approach through which dynamic models can be built and matched on real motions (analysis-synthesis approach).

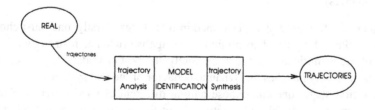

Figure 3: *Motion model identification.*

In this paper, *identification* is taken in the sense given by the theory of dynamical systems (i.e. identification of the parameters of a mathematical model), and not in the sense assumed in [EBBT93] (where motion identification referred to gesture interpretation). Similar problems were addressed in previous works such as [LPC95] where the coefficients of a mass-spring mesh were identified for realistic textile animation. The novelty of our work is to apply identification to living beings which involve complex control issues.

2 Theoretical Background in Identification

In this section we briefly present the theoretical framework of identification. Extensive works have been carried-out in the field of dynamic system identification over more than 50 years and good introductory textbooks or surveys are numerous (see for instance [KP71]). The following discussion is intended to be a minimal reminder of the related theory.

Conceptually, the dynamic behavior of a real physical system can be expressed, at least formally, by its so-called *evolution equation* (here the system is given in a time-discrete form, which is usually more suitable for computer simulations):

$$q(n+1) = f(q(n), u(n)), \tag{1}$$

where $u(n)$ is the *input vector* at time n. The so-called *state vector* $q(n)$ collects all the system's physical variables that matter for its evolution over time.

The aim of dynamic system modeling is to propose a mathematical model for f. In some cases, the primary motivation for such modeling is to investigate the system's properties (e.g. stability, determination of rate coefficients in chemical reactions). In other cases the interest is to design control strategies.

In a very general way, identification can be defined as follows :

- **Identification :** "Identification is the determination, on the basis of *input and output*, of a *model* within a specified *class of models*, to which the system under test is equivalent" [KP71].

- **Model :** Mathematical structure to which one tries to identify the system under test. One can utilize prior knowledge and physical insight about the system when selecting the model. A *class of models* refers to a family $\mathcal{F} = \{\mathcal{M}_\lambda, \lambda\}$ of models which share a common parametric structure (λ representing the model's parameters).

The identification process is performed in two stages. Firstly, one must choose an *appropriate* class of model. This preliminary stage is crucial as it strongly affects the outcome of the identification process. Secondly, the best candidate $\mathcal{M}_\lambda$ selected is the one that most closely matches the dynamic behavior of the real system.

For the first stage, one can choose among different classes of dynamic models, depending upon the available information about the system's behavior and structure [JHB+95] :

- **Physical modeling :** a model structure can be built on physical grounds, which has a certain number of parameters to be estimated from data.

- **Semi-physical modeling :** Physical insight is used to suggest certain non-linear combinations of measured data signal. These new signals are then subjected to model structures of black box character.

- **Black-box modeling :** No Physical insight is available or used, but the chosen model structure belongs to families that are known to have a good flexibility (e.g. neural networks).

Given the above definitions, let us see in more details how identification is actually performed once the class of models has been chosen. To fix notations, the dynamic model $\mathcal{M}_\lambda$ is characterized by its evolution equation, such as in equation 1 :

$$\hat{q}(n+1) = f_\lambda(\hat{q}(n), u(n)) \tag{2}$$

Here $\hat{q}$ refers to the state vector, as computed by the model $\mathcal{M}_\lambda$. One should not make the confusion between $\hat{q}$ and q (q refers to the actual state of the real system).

In the general case, q is not directly accessible by measurements and is observed through its outputs. The system's internal state then needs to be reconstructed from measurements, when possible. The observation of the system's behavior is performed by collecting time samples of the couples $(u(n), q(n))_{n \in [1,N]}$, where N is the total number of measurements.

The objective of identification is to compare the dynamic response of the real system to those of the model when operating in similar conditions (see figure 4). That is to say, to compare $q(n+1) = f(q(n), u(n))$ with $\hat{q}(n+1) = f_\lambda(q(n), u(n)), \forall n \in [1, N]$.

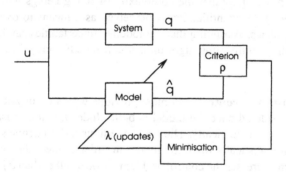

Figure 4: *Principle of dynamic system identification.*

Such a comparison can be made on several criteria, noted ρ. The chosen criterion depends on the studied problem and goals. A practical choice is to consider the Euclidean norm over R^N (where C is a diagonal scaling matrix):

$$\rho(q, \hat{q}) = \|C.(q - \hat{q})\|^2 = \sum_n c_n.(q(n) - \hat{q}(n))^2 \tag{3}$$

Identification can be stated and solved as an optimization problem (where variations on λ affect $\hat{q}$) :

$$\begin{cases} Min \; \rho(q, \hat{q}) \\ \lambda \end{cases} \qquad (4)$$

It must be pointed out that this presentation is far from exhaustive. This is only the minimal requirements for understanding the remainder of this paper. Let us now see how this framework can be applied for realistic animation of living beings.

3 Identification-minded Motion Modeling

Based on a cooperation between analysis and synthesis, motion identification recognizes the need to compare the model's behavior with real trajectories at some stage, and does it right from the beginning.

To support the view that identification requires a radically new way of thinking about dynamic models, one can list key differences with purely physics-based models.

3.1 Driving Principles

Semi-physical vs physical modeling. Physics-based modeling requires the creature to be physically (or at least "virtually") dissected, so that the actual mathematical structure can be built from modeling the individual components that contribute to motor control (including the skeleton, the flesh and the muscles, as well as the proprioceptive servoing and central pattern generator neural networks).

In the case of identification-minded modeling, emphasis is put on the motion to be produced rather than upon its observed dynamics, than on the physical constitution of the system. Acknowledging that the complexity of living beings will always escape modeling at some stage, identification is perceived as a means to overcome *a priori* modeling discrepancies. Assuming that unmodelled uncertainties can be compensated *a posteriori* by the identification algorithm, it can be advantageous to rely on semi-physical models.

A priori vs a posteriori control. In most previous works on physics-based modeling, control is considered once the model is built. Indeed, neuro-muscular control is not easily modeled mathematically. Thus, it is a tedious task to define subsequent control laws that can realistically drive the model in order to meet the animator's goals. The new approach addresses the control problem *a priori* rather than *a posteriori*. With semi-physical modeling, one is free to define generic mathematical equations which are not necessarily physically relevant, but which offer good properties. By restricting ourselves to build models from well-behaved differential equations, it is possible to prevent the model from undergoing unwanted or uncontrollable behaviors. Such equation sets can be very generic, provided the identification process can customize their behavior afterwards, so as to match real motions best.

Motion-dependent vs organism-dependent complexity. Traditionally, the complexity of a physics-based model is related to the "internal" (organic) structure of the considered system. The design process of physics-based modeling consists in making the equation set more and more complex, in an attempt to take phenomena and dynamic effects more accurately into account. One can ask oneself whether such a complexity is legitimate, especially when the performed motions are "simple". In computer graphics animation, is it not a nonsense to use models the complexity of which go far beyond the complexity of the motions they produce?

Whereas physics-based modeling puts much emphasis on the organic structure, identification-minded modeling focuses more on motion dynamics and on how to reproduce such behaviors at a minimal cost. Therefore the starting point when building the model should be : "what kind of dynamic behaviors are expected?" and not "which are the organic components and structure of the living being in question ?".

3.2 Modeling Guidelines

We now turn to more practical issues that need to be addressed when designing efficient dynamic models for identification :

(i) **Observability-guided decomposition :** Ultimately the model can be viewed as a single macro-block, whose inputs are the high-level commands and whose outputs are the degrees of freedom of the geometrical model. To tackle complexity through a divide-and-conquer approach, the motion under study is best decomposed as a set of "elementary" dynamic behaviors. Each of these motion building-bricks will be identified independently (provided one ensures that the couplings can be dealt-with afterwards [NAM97]). Physically complex motions emerge from the combined actions of individual organic components (neurons, muscles, flesh, skin, bones, etc). Here they are decomposed as a set of coupled functional blocks whose equivalent behavior can be observed through available measurements (proprioceptive feedback servoing, propulsion, interaction with the substrate, ...). It is crucial that each block be *observable*, i.e. that *information* provided by the experimental protocol be available and sufficient for its independent identification. For instance, one block can be split into two cascaded ones, whenever the interface between them can be observed.

(ii) **Intrinsic properties for "good" behaviors :** Each functional block is a dynamical system to be identified. When selecting the class of models, aptitude to match real observations is a major requirement. Other properties may be desirable. The form of the model can be chosen so as to prevent instabilities and uncontrollable behaviors to occur. Low computational cost is another feature that can be taken into account, right from the design stage.

(iii) **Suitability for successful identification :** When solving identification problems, the nature of the system's equations (e.g. non-linearities) strongly affects the efficiency and outcome of the chosen optimization scheme. Whenever possible, the structure of the specified class of models should take this into account.

To fix ideas, we shall now investigate how these general guidelines and driving principles can be applied to a practical case.

4 Illustration on a Study Case : Fish Locomotion

In order to illustrate the framework of motion identification, a pedagogic study case has been chosen. We were looking for a model sufficiently simple so that the mathematical equations could be developed extensively in order to provide the basis for a rigorous analysis and insight into how model properties and complexity actually affect the efficiency of the identification process. As a matter of fact, it is expected that applying the identification framework to more complex systems will eventually require complementary work-around solutions and increased user involvement. At this stage, extensive rigorous analysis are needed on a benchmark case. Given the extensive literature and comparative studies that can be already found on kinematic or dynamics-based fish motion [TT94, GT95, GTH98, NAHR95, NAM97], swim locomotion is particularly worth to investigate within the analysis-synthesis framework of identification. Moreover, swimming is not as simple as it may look at first glance, since it exhibits complexity in terms of non-linearities and couplings.

4.1 Experimental Protocol

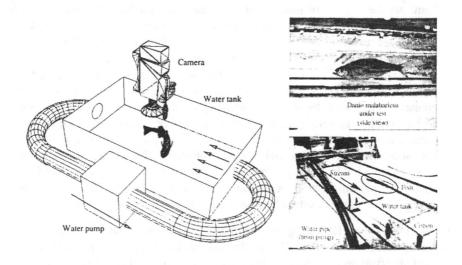

Figure 5: *Experimental protocol. Principle (left) and realization (right).*

In conventional motion capture sessions, the actor performs movements upon request. The actor can even repeat his motion until his performance has been successfully stored "in the box". This is not possible in our case. We can only *observe* the behavior of a real fish (Danio malabaricus) for a certain period of time, store the motion data and process them afterwards; but of course it is not possible to control the movement at will. Nevertheless, and whenever possible, the experimental set-up can be enhanced in order to ease the task of processing the motion data afterwards. The experimental workbench for motion analysis is depicted in figure 5.

By channeling a constant water flow stream produced by an electrical water pump, a constant external (exogenous) disturbance was applied to the fish. To compensate for the deviation, the animal needs to maintain the beat of its caudal fin, therefore constantly feeding the video with valuable motion data. At this early stage, the main focus was on studying planar motion (due to the caudal fin) which is more complex, while vertical motion (due to the pectoral fins which act as waterfoils) can be tackled independently [NAM97].

4.2 A Model Structure tailored for Identification

We shall now specify a suitable class of dynamic models for the swim motion. It has been built according to the general guidelines of section 3.

User commands consist of velocity and steering angle inputs. The model drives an articulated skeleton with seven segments, onto which a geometric skin is attached. From observing the dynamic behavior of the real fish, it appeared that it was appropriate to implement a finite-state machine to switch between forward swimming and turning (see figure 6).

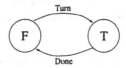

Figure 6: *The model embeds a finite-state machine to account for qualitatively different dynamics when the fish swims forward (F) or turns (T).*

The suggested model belongs to the general class of *hybrid* models, in the sense that it mixes discrete and continuous states. In our case, the two discrete states (swimming forward and turning) are associated with different dynamic behaviors, which can be identified separately.

Viewing fish motion as *impulse-driven* provides another means to decompose the model further. By observing the strokes (frequency and amplitude) delivered by the propelling caudal fin, and by relating those to the steering angle and average velocity, one gets insight into how the fish's displacement is achieved by a coordinated sequence of propelling impulses. This behavior is modeled as a functional block referred-to as the *impulse generator*.

Model decomposition can also distinguish between the motion of the fish considered as a rigid body, and the deformation of its skeleton. Rigid body motions are identified with a semi-physical model referred-to as the *hydrodynamic filter*, which accounts for fluid friction and the propelling effects of the caudal fin's strokes. Synchronously, the *deformation filter* directly relates articular angles of the skeleton to the frequency and amplitude delivered by the impulse generator. The model structure is given in figure 7.

This model complies with the idea of *observability-guided decomposition* (see section 3.2). Indeed, one can check that the inputs and outputs of each building block (impulse generator, hydrodynamic filter and deformation filter) can be measured on

54

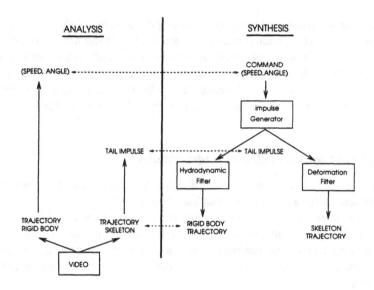

Figure 7: *Functional decomposition of the motion model exhibits several blocks whose individual dynamic behaviors can be observed and matched on the real fish.*

the real system for subsequent identification. At the lowest level, raw trajectories for rigid body motion and deformation are needed. To derive these data from the video sequence, standard image processing techniques were applied (image enhancement and shape extraction). Sophisticated image processing tailored for analyzing fish motion has been proposed in [LHW+91]. Progressively, higher level information can be obtained. Frequency and amplitude of the caudal fin beats can be deduced from the deformation. Moreover, getting average speed and steering angle (commands) involves several signal processings such as low-pass filtering the instantly observed speed and angle.

Intrinsic properties for "good behavior" are particularly visible on how efficient control is achieved. For instance, control laws implementation (in the impulse generator) can be made totally reliable and effective, by embedding additional constraint equations into the hydrodynamic model (see 14 in appendix. These constraints ensure that propelling impulses obey speed and angle commands.

Moreover, *suitability for identification* is particularly well illustrated by the hydrodynamic filter, as discussed in the next section.

4.3 Identification Process

Among the three blocks to be identified, the hydrodynamic filter is the more representative case. The model's equations are given in appendix for straight motion. These equations contain couplings and non-linearities with respect to the state variables.

By using the notations of section 2, one can write $q(n) = (\dot{\theta}(n), w(n), v(n))^\top$ and $u(n) = (\mathcal{A}(n), \varphi(n))^\top$ (θ is the orientation, while w and v are respectively the forward and lateral speeds, expressed in the local frame ; $\mathcal{A}$ and φ are the amplitude and instantaneous phasis of the impulses. See appendix for more details)

The form of the dynamic system can be written as :

$$\hat{q}(n+1) = f_\lambda(q(\hat{n}), u(n)) \tag{5}$$

In the above equation $\lambda \in R^5$ collects the model's parameters. The distance criterion is chosen as the Euclidean norm on R^N, where $(N+1)$ is the size of the experimental data set. We took the identity for the scaling matrix because each of state variables had values of the same magnitude order. The problem can be stated as:

$$\left\{ \begin{array}{l} Min \ \frac{1}{2}\sum_n[q(n+1) - \hat{q}(n+1)]^2 = \frac{1}{2}\sum_n[q(n+1) - f_\lambda(q(n), u(n))]^2 \\ \lambda \end{array} \right. \tag{6}$$

It can be seen that the system is linear with respect to the parameters (when function f_λ is viewed as a function of λ with $q(n)$, $A(n)$ and $\varphi(n)$ fixed). As a matter of fact, this property was forced to appear by appropriate parameterization. In order to prevent any confusion, it should be recalled that the dynamical system is non-linear with respect to the state vector (for instance check the term $\dot{\theta}(n)u(n)$ which appears in the model's equations). For a complete discussion on the respective concepts of *linearity in the parameters* and *linearity in dynamic behavior*, see [KP71].

Hence the system can be put in a matrix form:

$$A = \left(\begin{array}{cccccc} \dot{\theta}(1) & 0 & 0 & A(1)\sin(\varphi(1)) & 0 \\ 0 & w(1) - 2A(1)|\sin(\varphi(1))| & 0 & 0 & 0 \\ 0 & 0 & v(1) & 0 & A(1)\sin(\varphi(1)) \\ \vdots & \vdots & \vdots & \vdots & \vdots \\ \dot{\theta}(N) & 0 & 0 & A(N)\sin(\varphi(N)) & 0 \\ 0 & w(N) - 2A(N)|\sin(\varphi(N))| & 0 & 0 & 0 \\ 0 & 0 & v(N) & 0 & A(N)\sin(\varphi(N)) \end{array} \right) \tag{7}$$

and

$$B = \left(\begin{array}{c} \dot{\theta}(2) \\ w(2) - 2A(1)|\sin(\varphi(1))| - \dot{\theta}(1)v(1) \\ v(2) + \dot{\theta}(1)w(1) \\ \vdots \\ \dot{\theta}(N+1) \\ w(N+1) - 2A(N)|\sin(\varphi(N))| - \dot{\theta}(N)v(N) \\ v(N+1) + \dot{\theta}(N)w(N) \end{array} \right) \tag{8}$$

Equation 6 becomes

$$\left\{ \begin{array}{l} Min \ \frac{1}{2}\|A\lambda - B\|^2 \\ \lambda \end{array} \right. \tag{9}$$

In this case, the solution λ^* can be found by solving:

$$(A^T A)\lambda^* = A^T B \tag{10}$$

This equation provides the optimal parameter set, which ensures that the behavior of the dynamic model matches the real system as closely as possible. It can be seen that equation 10 is a pseudo-inverse formula, the solution of which can be obtained easily by solving the 5x5 linear system. Linearity in the parameters is a very valuable property of the suggested dynamic model. In the general (non-linear) case, identification would have relied on iterative algorithms such as Sequential Quadratic Programming for which convergence is not guaranteed. In our case, linearity ensures that the solution can be obtained in closed-form. It can thus be claimed that the suggested model complies with the guideline of "suitability for efficient identification" discussed in section 3.2.

4.4 Results

Acquisition of the complete sequence took about one and a half minutes, thereby building a motion data corpus of about 2250 samples (images) at 25Hz, among which 900 samples were processed. Meaningful sequences were those for which the fish exhibited behaviors that were not encountered before. Typically those meaningful segments (for instance the fish swimming at a given constant velocity) were about 100 sample long (4 seconds). Identification of the dynamic model's parameters λ requires that several beats (say 10) be observed.

The implementation code of the complete dynamic model features better than real-time performance. Dynamics are computed by SIMULINK/MATLAB[1] while 3D motion and skin deformation are performed by Alias|Wavefront's POWERANIMATOR [2], the two software packages communicating through UNIX sockets. The user can command the fish interactively. Swim motion of Danio malabaricus is reproduced to a level of quality which is very satisfying, given the computational cost. Images from figure 9 are extracted from an animation that can be viewed on the web (ftp://ftp.irisa.fr/local/siames /motion/IdentiFish.html).

5 Conclusion

The big shift from motion capture to identification comes from leaving a "motion trajectories in the box"-minded view, and going to a "motion dynamics in the box" way of thinking. Once identified, the user can freely drive the model. The living being may never have produced such motions during the observation stage. Still, synthetic motions would be performed in the fashion performed in reality. This approach requires a radically new way of thinking about motion dynamics and promotes a *motion-centric* rather than a *physics-centric* view on realistic animation.

Appendix : Dynamic equations for fish swim motion

Fish locomotion involves very complex hydrodynamic phenomena, because the interaction between the fish and water is two-way. For instance, pressure-induced forces and moments due to the forced harmonic motion of the fish body (and proportional to its acceleration) means that precise dynamics must take into account the concept of *added mass and inertia* [Fos94]. Also, it has been recently proved that tuna fish actually use active vorticity control for energy efficient locomotion [GTTB94].

---

[1] SIMULINK/MATLAB are registered trademarks of Mathworks Inc.

[2] POWERANIMATOR is a registered trademark of Alias|Wavefront, a subsidiary of Silicon Graphics Inc.

In order to study the mechanism of fish propulsion, we shall consider simplified rigid body dynamics (see figure 8). Let θ be the planar orientation of the fish with respect to the global frame. Let w and v be the local velocity vectors, respectively expressed with respect to the main and lateral axes.

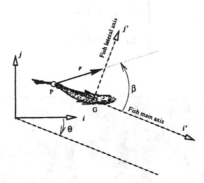

Figure 8: *Notations for rigid body hydrodynamics.*

As a simplifying approximation, the action-reaction principle suggests that:

$$F = -\xi \frac{dP}{dt} \tag{11}$$

where P represents the kinetic momentum of the expelled water quantity and ξ is an efficiency ratio. The kinetic momentum of the expelled quantity of water can be approximated by evaluating the volume $\mathcal{V}$ and velocity variation Δv of the quantity of water which is swept by the rotative motion of the caudal fin, say $\frac{dP}{dt} = \rho \sigma h \Delta v$, where ρ is the water density, σ the swept area, and h the average height of the caudal fin.

The *instantaneous phases* of the (quasi-periodic) deformation is defined as $\varphi(t) = 2\pi f(t)t$ where $f(t)$ is the frequency of the caudal fin beat. Let $\mathcal{A}(t)$ be the instantaneous amplitude of a single stroke. In [NAM97], it was shown that the actual shape of the propelling force can be approximated by considering its first harmonic component without significant loss of quality (higher harmonics being dampened by the hydrodynamic filter which is roughly "low-pass"). As a simplifying assumption, it is thus convenient to consider that the propelling pulse train is a sinewave for straight motion (more elaborate force profiles could be used with no restriction).Hence :

$$\left\{ \begin{array}{l} F(t)sin(\beta(t)) = k_1.\mathcal{A}(t).sin(\varphi(t)) \\ F(t)cos(\beta(t)) = k_2.\mathcal{A}(t).|sin(\varphi(t))| \end{array} \right. \tag{12}$$

Rigid-body hydrodynamics can be stated as :

$$\left\{ \begin{array}{l} J\ddot{\theta} = -\|\vec{PG}\|F(t)sin(\beta(t)) - \mu_\theta \dot{\theta} \\ m\dot{w} = F(t)cos(\beta(t)) - \mu_w w + m\dot{\theta}v \\ m\dot{v} = F(t)sin(\beta(t)) - \mu_v v - m\dot{\theta}w \end{array} \right. \tag{13}$$

where μ_θ, μ_w et μ_v are fluid friction coefficients. m represents the mass while J is the angular momentum.

It is possible to express the relationship between the amplitude $\mathcal{A}$ of a constant train of propelling impulses and the maintained average speed W.

$$\frac{k_2}{2}\mathcal{A} - \mu_w W = 0 \tag{14}$$

Imposing $\mathcal{A} = W$ yields to $\mu_w = \frac{k_2}{2}$ which removes one unknown parameter, while ensuring accurate control.

The model can be time-discretized by using the first-order Taylor formula ($\dot{f}(t) = \frac{f(t+dt)-f(t)}{dt}$), in which case the final equations are :

58

$$\begin{cases} \dot{\theta}(n+1) = \lambda_4.\mathcal{A}(n)sin(\varphi(n)) + \lambda_1\dot{\theta}(n) \\ w(n+1) = 2(1-\lambda_2).\mathcal{A}(n)|sin(\varphi(n))| + \lambda_2 w(n) + \dot{\theta}(n)v(n) \\ v(n+1) = \lambda_5.\mathcal{A}(n)sin(\varphi(n)) + \lambda_3 v(n) - \dot{\theta}(n)w(n) \end{cases} \quad (15)$$

where :

$$\begin{cases} \lambda_1 = 1 - \frac{\mu_\theta}{J} \\ \lambda_2 = 1 - \frac{\mu_w}{w} \\ \lambda_3 = 1 - \frac{\mu_v}{m} \\ \lambda_4 = \|\vec{PG}\|.\frac{k_1}{J} \\ \lambda_5 = \frac{k_1}{m} \end{cases} \quad (16)$$

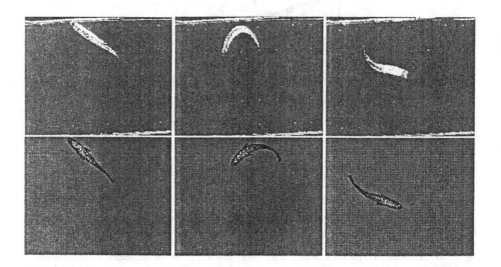

Figure 9: *A dynamic model has been designed with the idea of carrying subsequent identification proces ses in mind. For efficient model design, simplified dynamics (semi-physical model) are considered and desirable properties su ch as real-time performance, controllability and stability prevail over the strict physical relevance of the biomechanical mo del. The identification process minimizes model imperfections afterwards, by tuning parameters in order to obtain the best ma tch with the dynamic behavior of a real fish.*

References

[BRRP97]   B. Bodenheimer, C. Rose, S. Rosenthal, and J. Pella. The process of motion capture: Dealing with the data. In *Eurographics Workshop on Computer Animation and Simulation*, pages 3–18, September 1997.

[BW95]   A. Bruderlin and L. Williams. Motion signal-processing. *Computer Graphics*, pages 97–108, July 1995. In proceedings of ACM SIGGRAPH'95.

[Coh92]   M. Cohen. Interactive spacetime control for animation. *Computer Graphics*, 24(2):293–302, July 1992.

[EBBT93]   L. Emerging, R. Boulic, S. Balcisoy, and D. Thalmann. Computer-aided design of a generic robot controller handling reactivity and real-time control issues. *IEEE Transactions on Control Systems Technology*, 1(4), 1993.

[Fos94]   T. Fossen. *Guidance and Control of Ocean Vehicles*. John Wiley & sons, 1994.

[GR96]   S. Guo and J. Roberge. A high-level control mechanism for human locomotion based on para-
            metric frame space interpolation. In *Eurographics Workshop on Computer Animation and Sim-
            ulation*, pages 95–107, Poitiers, France, September 1996. Springer Verlag.

[GT95]   R. Grzeszczuk and D. Terzopoulos. Automated learning of muscle-actuated locomotion trough
            control abstraction. *Proceedings of ACM SIGGRAPH '95*, pages 63–70, August 1995.

[GTH98]   R. Grzeszczuk, D. Terzopoulos, and G. Hinton. Neuroanimator: Fast neural network emulation
            and control of physics-based models. *Proceedings of ACM SIGGRAPH '98*, August 1998.

[GTTB94]   R. Gopalkrishnan, G.S. Triantafyllou, M.S. Tryantafillou, and D. Barrett. Active vorticity con-
            trol in a shear flow using a flapping foil. *Journal of Fluid Mechanics*, 274:1–21, 1994.

[HBWO95]   J. Hodgins, D. Brogan, W. Wooten, and J. O'Brien. Animating human athletics. *Proceedings of
            ACM SIGGRAPH '95*, pages 71–77, August 1995.

[Hod96]   J. Hodgins. Three-dimensional human running. *Proceedings of the IEEE Conference on
            Robotics and Automation*, 1996.

[JHB+95]   A. Juditsky, H. Hjalmarsson, A. Benveniste, B. Delyon, L. Ljung, J. Sjöberg, and Q. Zhang.
            Nonlinear black-box models in system identification : Mathematical foundations. *Automatica*,
            32(12):1725–1550, 1995.

[KB93]   H. Ko and N.I. Badler. Straight line walking animation based on kinematic generalization that
            preserves the original characteristics. In *Graphics Interface*, pages 9–16, Toronto, Ontario,
            Canada, May 1993.

[KB96]   H. Ko and N. I. Badler. Animating human locomotion in real-time using inverse dynamics.
            IEEE Computer Graphics & Applications, 1996.

[KP71]   K.J.Astrom and P.Eykhoff. System identification - a survey. *Automatica*, 7:123–162, 1971.

[LHW+91]   C. Lee, O. Hasegawa, W. Wongwaraaipat, H. Dohi, and M. Ishizuka. Realistic image synthesis
            of a deformable living thing based on motion understanding. *Journal of Visual Communication
            and Image Representation*, pages 345–354, 1991.

[LPC95]   JL. Louchet, X. Provot, and D. Crochemore. Evolutionary identification of cloth animation mod-
            els. In Springer-Verlag, editor, *Sixth EUROGRAPHICS workshop on animation and simulation,
            Maastricht,The Netherlands*, Sept 1995.

[MBT96]   T. Molet, R. Boulic, and D. Thalmann. A real time anatomical converter for human motion
            capture. In *Eurographics Workshop on Computer Animation and Simulation*, pages 79–94,
            September 1996.

[NAHR95]   J.L. Nougaret, B. Arnaldi, G. Hegron, and A. Razavi. Quick tuning of a reference locomotion
            gait. In *Proceedings of Computer Animation '95. IEEE editor. Geneva*, April 1995.

[NAM97]   J.L. Nougaret, B. Arnaldi, and F. Multon. Coarse-to-fine design of feedback controllers for
            dynamic locomotion. *The Visual Computer*, 1(13):435–455, 1997.

[NM93]   J.T. Ngo and J. Marks. Spacetime constraints revisited. *Proceedings of ACM SIGGRAPH '93*,
            pages 343–350, August 1993.

[Ren94]   S. Renous. *Locomotion*. Dunod, Paris, 1994.

[RGBC96]   C. Rose, B. Guenter, B. Bodenheimer, and M.F. Cohen. Efficient generation of motion transi-
            tions using spacetime constraints. In *Proceedings of ACM SIGGRAPH*, pages 147–154, New
            Orelans, Louisiana, August 1996. Addison Wesley.

[TT94]   X. Tu and D. Terzopoulos. Artificial fishes: Physics, locomotion, perception, behavior. *Com-
            puter Graphics*, pages 43–50, August 1994. In proceedings of ACM SIGGRAPH'94.

[UAT95]   M. Unuma, K. Anjyo, and R. Takeuchi. Fourier principles for emotion-based human figure ani-
            mation. *Computer Graphics*, pages 91–96, July 1995. In proceedings of ACM SIGGRAPH'95.

[vdP96]   M. van de Panne. Parametrized gait synthesis. *IEEE Computer Graphics and Applications*,
            pages 12–27, March 1996.

[vdPF93]   M. van de Panne and E. Fiume. Sensor-actuator networks. *Proceedings of ACM SIGGRAPH
            '93, ACM Computer Graphics*, pages 335–342, August 1993.

Interactive Solid Animation Using Linearized Displacement Constraints

François Faure
Institut für Computergrafik
Technische Universität, Wien

Abstract. We present a new approach for interactive solid animation. It allows a user to efficiently trade-off accuracy for speed, making complicated structures tractable in interactive time. Linearized displacement constraints are used in conjunction with an efficient iterative equation solver to perform the assembly of articulated solids. This allows the initialization of a scene and the correction of numerical integration errors. A robust integration scheme limits the instabilities due to approximations. Applications are shown and discussed.

1 Introduction

Interactivity is a major issue in computer animation. However, interactive articulated solid animation has yet been restricted to small structures, except in special cases. This lack of interactivity may be due to the inheritance of the computer animation techniques from robotics and mechanical engineering. The primary concern of these sciences is physical accuracy rather than computation time. Fast applications such as robot control are applied to simple structures, compared with the objects we want to animate in computer graphics. Virtual reality and large interactive applications require a new approach based on the control of the computation time. Experiments show that when dragging an object, users prefer quick responses, even with low precision, than waiting a few seconds for a precise motion. This implies trading-off accuracy for speed. This idea has been extensively used for rendering. The specific problem of animation is the possible accumulation of error over time, leading to inacceptable results. Therefore, we present an approach based on fast structure assembly and stable integration scheme. By performing the assembly at the end of each time step just before displaying the scene, one can accept relatively large errors inside the time step. This tolerance allows the approximate computation of the time derivatives and the use of large time steps in the numerical integration. As a result, interactivity can be obtained for large scenes.

The remainder of this paper is organized as follows. In section 2, we briefly describe the problems of time integration applied to the simulation of articulated structures, and how they have been dealt with in the field of computer graphics. We then present an alternative approach well-known in mechanical simulation, which seems currently unused in our domain. The following sections present variants of this approach that we have developed in order to meet the needs of computer graphics. Section 3 describes an assembly algorithm for complex articulated structures. Section 4 presents applications to animation such as inverse kinematics, dynamics, along with first results in trading-off accuracy for speed in computer animation.

2 Background and motivation

Numerical simulation consists in integrating a differential equation over time. From a practical point of view, this requires repeatedly computing the time derivative of the system, and integrating it over a (possibly variable) time step. The laws of physics provide equations on accelerations, which allow the animation of systems of particules as ordinary differential equations (ODEs). In contrast, constrained systems such as articulated structures include joints with associated geometrical equations which must remain satisfied over time. This leads form ODEs to differential algebraic equations (DAEs), which are more difficult to handle. The DAE governing a physically-based articulated body can be expressed in matrix form as:

$$\dot{q} = Dv \tag{1}$$
$$M\dot{v} = f(t, q, v) + J^T(q)\lambda \tag{2}$$
$$0 = g(t, q) \tag{3}$$

where q is the set of coordinates, M the mass matrix associated with the coordinates, f represents the external forces, g the geometrical constraints, and J the derivative of g with respect to the coordinates, also called the Jacobian of the constraints. Matrix D relates the velocities to the derivatives of the coordinates, e.g. angular velocity to quaternion derivatives. The exponent T represents matrix transposition. The vector λ gathers the independent components of the constraint forces, acting along the directions of the geometrical constraints. In the remaining of the paper, we use bold letters to denote global vectors and matrices, gathering values related to all the joints or solids of the articulated bodies.

Differentiating twice equation (3) and substituting into equation (2) provides

$$\ddot{g} = JM^{-1}(f + J^T\lambda) + a_v = 0 \tag{4}$$

where a_v is the velocity-dependent part of the relative accelerations. Solving equation (4) provides the constraint forces λ, then the time derivatives through equations (2) and (1). Using the derivatives, we can compute a new position using:

$$x(t + dt) = x(t) + \phi(t, x(t), dt)$$

where ϕ represents an integration scheme such as Euler or Runge-Kutta. Unfortunately, all integration schemes introduce more or less drift, i.e. equation (3) and its first derivative are no more satisfied at time $t + dt$, even if we start from a consistent state at time t. This drift eventually results in solids moving apart from each other without meeting the joint constraints, and it can quickly become visible. The drift is restricted to loop closures if relative coordinates are used.

In order to keep the drift within reasonable values, *Baumgarte stabilization* is very popular[3, 2, 8]. It consists in using a modified version of equation (4), namely:

$$\ddot{g} = JM^{-1}(f + J^T\lambda) + a_v = \gamma_1\dot{g} + \gamma_2 g$$

where γ_1 and γ_2 are parameters provided by the user, and the vectors g and $\dot{g}$ straightforwardly computable at each time step. This perturbation acts much like damped springs applied to each constraint. This method has also shown capabilities of assembling articulated solids[2]. Unfortunately, the values of γ_1 and γ_2 are difficult to set. Too weak, they do not prevent the drift from reaching inacceptable values. Too high, they induce instabilities due to time sampling. The optimal compromise can be very difficult to find. In many cases, the stiffness induced by this method makes the use of small time steps necessary, thus reducing the computational efficiency.

More recently, efficient alternative approaches have been proposed, introducing the principle of *post-stabilization*[1, 4]. The basic idea is to proceed in two steps:

- starting from $(q(t), v(t))$, integrate the velocities and accelerations over the time interval dt using your favorite integration scheme, e.g. Runge-Kutta, and denote the result $(\tilde{q}(t + dt), \tilde{v}(t + dt))$

- perform *post-stabilization* in order to meet the geometric constraints and their first derivatives:

$$
\begin{aligned}
q(t + dt) &= \tilde{q}(t + dt) - \delta q & (5) \\
v(t + dt) &= \tilde{v}(t + dt) - \delta v & (6)
\end{aligned}
$$

The computation of the correction terms is explained in section 3.3. This approach frees the user from tuning arbitrary stabilization parameters, and experiments have shown better stability than Baumgarte stabilization[4]. The authors show that if the truncation error of the integration scheme is $O(dt^{p+1})$ then the drift is $O(dt^{2(p+1)})$.

In this paper, we provide three contributions to this approach. First, we generalize the position stabilization (eq.5) to an iterative assembly algorithm. This allows the automatic initialization of scenes including complex geometric constraints.

Second, we include the assembly method in a simple integration scheme which makes no explicit use of velocity. This avoids performing the velocity stabilization (eq.6), which results in more computational efficiency. This also avoids us to derive noisy input data such as coordinates of 3D trakers.

Finally, we investigate the capabilities of post-stabilization for purposes of interactivity instead of precision. It is commonly admitted in mechanical engineering that the fourth-order Runge-Kutta integration scheme is the most efficient in most practical cases[10]. This requires computing four derivatives at each time step. Performing standard post-stabilization requires two additional dynamic solutions. Our approach is particularly useful when, for purposes of interactivity, we can not afford even *one* dynamic solution within an animation step.

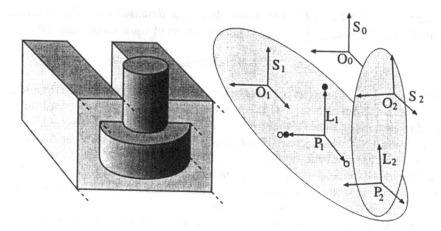

Figure 1: Our model applied to a joint with one translation and one rotation allowed. The two reference frames of this joint are centered on P_1 and P_2, with their direction aligned with the main axes of the joint. The solids are centered on O_1 and O_2, and the absolute coordinate system on O_0. The full and empty disks respectively denote translation and rotation constraints.

3 Fast assembly of articulated structures

Structure assembly can be used either to initialize complicated scenes including closed loops, or to correct positions after time integration. We first present our joint model, which allows us to compute geometric constraints for a wide variety of joints. We then show how to obtain a linearized geometric equation by writing it as a kinematic equation. Then we turn the non-square kinematic equation system into a square dynamics equation system. We finally describe the assembly algorithm.

3.1 Joint model and kinematic equations

We consider two solids represented by their local frames S_1 and S_2 centered on O_1 and O_2, respectively. An example is shown in figure 1. The positions of the solids are defined with respect to a reference frame (O_0, S_0). Let the solids be bound by a joint L_{12}. We represent this joint using two local frames L_1 and L_2 attached to S_1 and S_2 and centered in P_1 and P_2, respectively. The geometric constraints between L_1 and L_2 define the type of the joint. A universal joint requires P_1 and P_2 to remain equal, whereas a plane-to-plane joint requires that one plane fixed in L_1 coincides with one plane fixed in L_2.

The velocities have to be consistent with the constraints. For simplicity, a good choice is to express the kinematic equations at the center of one of the joint frames, this frame being aligned with the motion constraints. Expressing the relative velocity between solids S_i and S_j at point P_i provides:

$$
\begin{aligned}
v_{ij} &= v_i(P_i) - v_j(P_j) \\
&= v_i(O_i) + \omega_i \times O_iP_i - v_j(O_j) - \omega_j \times (O_jP_j + P_jP_i) \\
\omega_{ij} &= \omega_i - \omega_j
\end{aligned}
$$

Table 1: Kinematic constraints associated with different types of joints. A cross denotes the presence of a kinematic constraint along the associated direction. Translation and rotation directions are denoted using em t and em r, respectively. We chose arbitrarily the vector i as the main axis of the joint.

joint type	ti	tj	tk	ri	rj	rk
universal	×	×	×			
pin	×	×	×		×	×
cylindrical		×	×		×	×
prismatic		×	×	×	×	×
ball-socket		×	×			
smooth surface contact	×					

The kinematics equations associated with a joint including n_t translation constraints and n_r rotation constraints can be written as:

$$v_{ij}(P).t_k = \dot{c}_k \quad 1 \le k \le n_t \tag{7}$$

$$\omega_{ij}.r_k = \dot{c}_k \quad n_t < k \le n_t + n_r \tag{8}$$

where t_k and r_k are translation and rotation constraint directions. The scalars $\dot{c}$ are the values of the velocity constraints in translation or rotation. These values are null for perfect joints. Table (1) shows the kinematic constraints associated with some common joints. Further work will include dependent constraint directions such as screws.

Generally, there is a whole space of velocities consistent with the constraints, and we want to compute the consistent velocities which are the nearest to given values. The sets of equations (7,8) related to all the joints of the scene can thus be gathered in the following matrix equation:

$$J\delta v = \dot{c} - Jv \tag{9}$$

where v is the current global velocity vector and δv is a velocity correction necessary to reach the space of consistent velocitites. The solution of the equation system is explained in section 3.3. Using relative coordinates, only the loop closures require the solution of a kinematic equation, the acyclic constraints being implicitly satisfied.

3.2 Linearized geometric equations

Starting from an inconsistent state, we want to compute new positions satisfying the geometric constraints. Geometric equations are generally difficult to solve because they involve nonlinear equations including sine functions. We obtain a linear equation by integrating a kinematic equation over a virtual time step dt^*:

$$J\delta v dt^* = b \tag{10}$$

where b is the displacement constraints necessary to cancel the errors. We explain at the end of this section how to compute the displacement constraints. The solution of the equation provides the unknown vector $\delta v dt^*$. The coordinate corrections are straight-forwarly obtained using equation (1):

$$\delta q = D \delta v dt^*$$

The solution of the linearized equation system is good approximation of the real solution when small displacements are involved. We do not explicitly use the virtual time step since its value is arbitrary.

Now we show a simple way of computing the displacement constraint . This requires representing the relative rotation of the two joint coordinate frames as $\omega_{ij} dt^*$. The relative translation δ_{ij} and the relative rotation $R(L_i, L_j)$ can be computed using transitivity:

$$\delta_{ij} = P_i P_j = P_i O_i + O_i O + O O_j + O_j P_j$$
$$R(L_i, L_j) = R(L_i, S_i) . R(S_i, S_0) . R(S_0, S_j) . R(S_j, L_j)$$

where the operator R is your favorite rotation model (quaternions, matrices, Euler angles...) and the dot denotes the appropriate transitivity operator. We then turn the relative rotation into an (axis,angle) form where the axis is a unit vector, and finally turn it into a three dimensional vector defined as the axis multiplied by the angle, that we call $\bar{\omega}_{ij}$. Projecting the relative rotation and translation to the corresponding constraint directions provides the values of the geometric constraint errors. The displacement constraints are, for each joint, the opposite of the geometric errors:

$$b_k = -\delta_{ij} . t_k \quad 1 \le k \le n_t$$
$$b_k = -\bar{\omega}_{ij} . r_k \quad n_t < k \le n_t + n_r$$

3.3 From kinematics to dynamics

Since the number of constraints is independent on the number of coordinates, the Jacobian matrix is typically non-square. A way of regularizing the equation system is to use constraint forces to move the solids. This leads from kinematics to dynamics. In dynamics, each solid S_i obeys the fundamental principle:

$$f_i = M_i \dot{v}_i \tag{11}$$

where f_i and $\ddot{q}_i$ are six-dimensional vectors denoting force and acceleration, and M_i the mass matrix of S_i. A common assumption about constraint forces is that they act along the constraint axes. This derives from the principle of virtual works applied to perfect joints. In this case, the forces applied to the solids by the constraints are simply $J^T \lambda$ where the vector λ gathers all the constraint forces. This leads to the equation system:

$$\begin{pmatrix} M & -J^T \\ -J & 0 \end{pmatrix} \begin{pmatrix} \delta \dot{v} \\ \lambda \end{pmatrix} = \begin{pmatrix} 0 \\ -b \end{pmatrix} \tag{12}$$

where the first line is Newton's law restricted to the constraint forces, and the second line is the kinematics equation. Vector b is the relative acceleration correction. It is the opposite of the relative acceleration which would occur along constrained directions if null constraint forces were applied. Vector λ represents the unknown constraint forces necessary to enforce the kinematic constraints. They result in an acceleration correction $\delta\dot{v}$. The equation system (12) is square and models physical interactions between the solids. Absolute coordinates involve a diagonal mass matrix, whereas relative coordinates require computing the entries of a dense matrix. In both cases, matrix M is symmetric positive definite. It is thus possible to perform a substitution of the first line into the second one to obtain a new, reduced equation system:

$$A\lambda = b, \quad with \ A = JM^{-1}J^T \tag{13}$$

The corrections can then be computed as

$$\delta\dot{v} = M^{-1}J^T(JM^{-1}J^T)^{-1}b$$

Note that using the identity as a mass matrix is equivalent with performing a left pseudo-inverse solution, well-known in kinematics[6]. This is our motivation for performing a dynamic solution: it is a straightforward generalization of the standard kinematics approaches, and it allows us to compute physically realistic motions. Corrections of velocities or positions are computed in a similar way when performing post-stabilization.

3.4 The fast assembly algorithm

Starting from a state q, the assembly is performed by adding to vector q an increment δq computed by the function *correction*. This function, which pseudocode is given below, computes iteratively a position correction necessary to meet the constraints. At each iteration, it solves a linear system similar with equation (12), except that position corrections are computed instead of acceleration corrections. This linear system is a fist-order approximation of the geometric equations. Several iterations may thus be necessary. The computation of the correction terminates as soon as a displacement satisfying all the geometric constraints up to a given precision has been computed. This is checked by the boolean function *geometryOk*. The algorithm can also terminate after a given number of iteration have been performed. The procedure *compute_entries* computes the entries of matrices M, J and the displacement constraint b corresponding to given coordinates.

```
correction(q){
    δq = 0
    compute_entries( q, M, J, b )
    while not geometryOk( b ){
        δq += M⁻¹Jᵀ(JM⁻¹Jᵀ)⁻¹b
        compute_entries( q + δq, M, J, b )
    }
    return δq
}
```

In contrast with differential approaches[2, 7], our assembly process is not delayed through time and thus allows the display of accurate geometry at any animation step. In

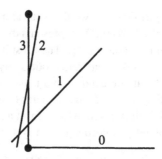

Figure 2: Example of convergence of the assembly method. The geometric constraints state that the endpoints of the bar have to coincide with the centers of the disks.

contrast with kinematical approaches[6, 11], it makes use of mass and it is thus compatible with dynamics.

In practice, the convergence of the algorithm is fast (see example in figure 2), except if the rotations reach high values. In this case the linear approximation is too poor and the system may enter an endless process. To solve this problem, we simply truncate excessive rotations. Empirically, 0.8 radians seems a good value.

At each iteration, the linear equation equation (13) is solved using the biconjugate gradient algorithm[9]. Instead of computing explicitly a decomposition of the matrix $JM^{-1}J^T$, the algorithm solves the equation system by performing a sequence of matrix products. Using absolute coordinates allows the use of matrix sparsity, providing a good efficiency. The biconjugate gradient algorithm performs an iterative minimization of the error. This allows the termination of the algorithm to occur as soon as the desired precision is reached, using various norms, or after a given number of iterations have been performed. Moreover, this algorithm handles indefinite equation systems, and computes a least-square solution in case of inconsistent constraints.

The computation of the correction is twice iterative: each loop traversal involves an iterative solution of a linear equation system. Limiting the number of iterations allow the user to trade-off accuracy for speed, which is useful when applied to complex structures. An example of complex assembly is shown in figure (3). This scenes includes 758 scalar constraints. Six iterations aree used to perform the assembly, each of them limited to 30 conjugate gradient iterations. The computation time is less than one second on a standard SGI O2 workstation.

4 Applications to animation

4.1 Inverse kinematics

We apply our articulated body method to a VR environment including 3D hand-trackers with buttons. This allows us to interactively catch, drag and release objects. A straightforward application is inverse kinematics. A joint binding the tracker and the solid pointed by the traker is created when the button is clicked. As long as the button remains pressed, the position and orientation of the joint is updated according to the position of the traker. Applying the assembly algorithm allows the structure to "follow" the tracker

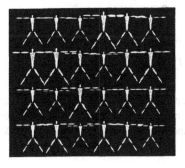 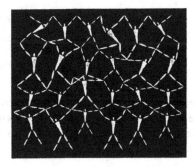

Figure 3: Complex assembly. We want to bind the hands and feet of the different-sized characters.

according to the geometric constraints. A null inverse mass is applied to the tracker, so that only the other objects can be corrected.

4.2 Dynamics

In dynamics, the forces are responsible for the accelerations of the solids. The velocities remain unchanged in case of null forces. So far, we have not yet introduced velocities in the system. Velocities are difficult to compute from 3D traker input since the trackers generally measure only positions. Numerical derivation is dangerous because noisy data induce instability. The problem is even harder when dealing with accelerations. Filtering the data is not a satisfying solution because it introduces disturbing delays. To avoid this problem, we apply Stoermer's integration scheme[9], which makes no explicit use of velocities, using the previous displacements Δq instead. This integration scheme can be written as:

$$\Delta q(t + dt) = \Delta q(t) + \ddot{q}dt^2$$
$$q(t + dt) = q(t) + \Delta q(t + dt)$$

This integration scheme requires an initialization of Δq, e.g. $\Delta q(0) = \dot{q}(0)dt + \frac{1}{2}dt^2\ddot{q}$. It fits perticularly well with our assembly approach. We perform the assembly at the end of each time step so that the geometric errors arising from numerical integration are canceled before displaying the scene. The position increment vector is updated as well as the positions themselves. The pseudocode for a simulation step is as follows:

```
step( dt ){
    Δq += M⁻¹fdt²
    q  += Δq
    δq  = correction(q)
    q  += δq
    Δq += δq
}
```

Note the extreme simplicity of this animation scheme. We do not even compute accelerations compatible with the constraints. Rather, only external forces are considered

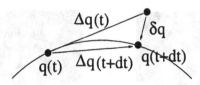

Figure 4: Our method applied to a simple example. A particle is constrained to remain on a fixed circle. It first moves according to its previous motion (in this example, there are no external forces applied). Then a correction δq is applied in order to meet the constraint. The displacement Δq is updated accordingly.

in vector f, the solid first move as if they were free, and their positions (and displacements) are corrected at the end of each time step. This results in correcting simultaneously acceleration and numerical integration errors, and allows performing large time steps. An illustration is shown in figure 4. Note that the updated "velocity" is the displacement between two positions compatible with the constraints. Contrary with Baumgarte stabilization, this method induces few velocity in the directions of the geometrical constraints. As a result, the method is much more robust to large time steps.

Compared with previous related work[5], the efficiency of our method comes from the use of the biconjugate gradient algorithm, along with a robust integration scheme.

We validated this integration scheme using numerous experiments involving isolated articulated bodies. Energy and momentum remain constant up to machine roundoff precision. Bodies linked to the ground may suffer from energy variations, similarly with what happens using other integration schemes. The limits of this approach are reached when strong forces generate large displacements requiring large corrections. In this case, numerical roundoffs and linear approximations may result in jerky motion, unless short time steps are used. Further work will include acceleration correction.

4.3 Trading-off accuracy for speed

Interactivity is necessary in applications such as virtual reality. Our iterative approach allows the user to tune the level of interactivity by limiting the computation time. The number of assembly iterations can be set to one for high interactivity, while three are generally enough for high precision. The number of conjugate gradient iterations can often be reduced to a surprisingly small number compared with the theoretical number, which is equal to (at most) the number of constraints. Applied to the articulated structure in figure 5 including 56 solids and 261 scalar constraints, 2 geometrical iterations each of them involving 5 conjugate gradient iterations allow us to drag the structure interactively. In contrast, 3 geometrical iterations each of them involving 50 conjugate gradient iterations are necessary to obtain a visually perfect geometric accuracy, resulting in poor interactivity.

Large time steps allow the use of real-world time. In our application, time is read at each entry in the main animation loop, and the time step is deduced from the time of the previous entry. Due to various technical reasons, this time step is not constant. The previous displacements Δq used by the integration scheme are scaled by dividing the new time step by the previous one. Since the different time steps have the same order of mag-

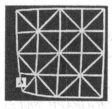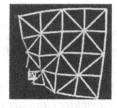

Figure 5: Interactive positioning. Low geometrical precision allows interactivity during motion. Precision is eventually recovered.

Figure 6: Interactive dynamics. The user shakes the plate using a 3D tracker. Low precision allows high interactivity with visually correct results.

nitude, the division does not induce important roundoff errors. We were able to animate the scene shown in figure 6 at 12 frames per second on a standard SGI O2 workstation. This scene includes 28 solids and 108 scalar constraints. Only one geometric iteration and fifteen conjugate gradient iterations are performed for each animation frame. The rendering takes approximately half the computation time.

5 Future work

Our modified post-stabilization approach with tunable accuracy or computation time has shown good capabilities for interactive solid animation. Further improvements should include initial guesses of the conjugate gradient solution. However, we have found few similarity between constraint forces from one step to another using displacement constraints. We expect to find more temporal coherency using acceleration correction. Valuable initial guesses may allow the rapid computation of accelerations more compatible with the constraints. This would reduce the geometrical error at each step and consequently, the number of stabilization iterations. Additionally, weighting the geometric errors in terms of their contribution to the percepted accuracy may reduce the necessary computations.

Aknowledgements

We gratefully acknowledge the support of the European Union's Training and Mobility of Researchers (TMR) programme in funding this work.

References

1. U. M. Ascher, H.Chin, L.R.Petzold, and S. Reich. Stabiliation of constrained mechanical systems with daes and invariant manifold. *Journal of Mechanics of Structures and Machines*, 23(2):135–157, 1995.

2. Ronen Barzel and Alan H. Barr. A modeling system based on dynamic constraints. In John Dill, editor, *Computer Graphics (SIGGRAPH '88 Proceedings)*, volume 22, pages 179–188, August 1988.

3. J. Baumgarte. Stabilization of constraints and integrals of motion in dynamical systems. *Computer Methods in Applied Mechanics*, 1:1–36, 1972.

4. Hong Sheng Chin. *Stabilization Methods for Simulations of Constrained Multibody Dynamics*. PhD thesis, University of British Columbia, 1995.

5. M.P. Gascuel and J.D. Gascuel. Displacement constraints for interactive modeling and animation of articulated structures. *The Visual Computer*, 10(4):191–204, March 1994.

6. Michael Girard and Anthony A. Maciejewski. Computational modeling for the computer animation of legged figures. In B. A. Barsky, editor, *Computer Graphics (SIGGRAPH '85 Proceedings)*, volume 19, pages 263–270, July 1985.

7. M. Gleicher. *A Differential Approach to Graphical Manipulation*. PhD thesis, Carnegie Mellon University, 1994.

8. Paul M. Isaacs and Michael F. Cohen. Mixed methods for complex kinematic constraints in dynamic figure animation. *The Visual Computer*, 4(6):296–305, December 1988.

9. Press, Teukolski, Vetterling, and Flannery. *Numerical Recipes in C*. Cambridge University Press, 1992.

10. W. Schielen. *Multibody Systems Handbook*. Springer, Berlin, 1990.

11. Jianmin Zhao and Norman I. Badler. Inverse kinematics positioning using nonlinear programming for highly articulated figures. *ACM Transactions on Graphics*, 13(4):313–336, October 1994.

Modeling Objects for Interaction Tasks

Marcelo Kallmann and Daniel Thalmann

EPFL Computer Graphics Lab – LIG
CH-1015 – Lausanne – Switzerland
{kallmann, thalmann}@lig.di.epfl.ch

Abstract. This paper presents a new approach to model general interactions between virtual human agents and objects in virtual worlds. The proposed framework is designed to deal with many of the possible interactions that may arise while simulating a virtual human performing common tasks in a virtual environment. The idea is to include within the object description, all the necessary information to describe how to interact with it. For this, a feature modeling approach is used, by means of a graphical user interface program, to identify object interaction features. Moving parts, functionality instructions and interaction locations are examples of some considered features. Following this approach, the control of the simulation is decentralized from the main animation control, in the sense that some local instructions on how to deal with the object are encapsulated within the object itself. To illustrate the approach, some examples are shown and discussed.

1 Introduction

The necessity to model interactions between an object and a virtual human agent (here after just referred to as an agent), appears in most applications of computer animation and simulation. Such applications encompass several domains, as for example: virtual autonomous agents living and working in virtual environments, human factors analysis, training, education, virtual prototyping, and simulation-based design. A good overview of such areas is presented by Badler [2]. An example of an application using agent-object interactions is presented by Johnson et al [12], whose purpose is to train equipment usage in a populated virtual environment.

Commonly, simulation systems perform agent-object interactions for specific tasks. Such approach is simple and direct, but most of the time, the core of the system needs to be updated whenever one needs to consider another class of objects.

Autonomous agent applications try to model agent's knowledge using recognition, learning and understanding techniques from information retrieved through sensors [15]. Agent's knowledge is then used to solve all possible interactions with an object. Even in such a case, some information of intrinsic object functionality must be provided. Consider the example of opening a door: just the rotation movement of the door is provided a priori. All other actions should be planned by agents knowledge: walking to reach the door, searching for a knob, deciding which hand to use, moving body limbs to reach the knob, deciding which hand posture to use, turning the knob, and finally opening the door. This simple example illustrates how complex it can be to perform a simple agent-object interaction task.

To overcome such difficulties, a natural way is to include within the object description, more useful information than only intrinsic object properties. Some proposed systems already use this kind of approach. In particular, the *object specific reasoning* [13] creates a relational table to inform object purpose and, for each object graspable site, the appropriate hand shape and grasp approach direction. This set of information may be sufficient to perform a grasping task, but more information is needed to perform different types of interactions.

This paper describes a framework to model general agent-object interactions based on objects containing interaction information of various kinds: intrinsic object properties, information on how-to-interact with it, object behaviors, and also expected agent behaviors. Compared to the work of Levinson [13], our approach extends the idea of having a database of interaction information. For each object modeled, we include the functionality of its moving parts and detailed commands describing each desired interaction, by means of a dedicated script language.

A feature modeling approach [21] is used to include all desired information in objects. A graphical interface program permits the user to interactively specify different features in the object, and save them as a script file. We call such an object, modeled with its interaction features, as *Smart Object*.

The adjective *smart* has been used in a number of different contexts. For instance, Russel et al [18] and Pentland [17] discuss interactive spaces instrumented with cameras and microphones to perform audio-visual interpretation of human users. This capacity of interpretation made them *smart spaces*. In our case, an object is called *smart* when it has the ability to describe its possible interactions.

A parallel with the object oriented programming paradigm can also be made in the sense that each object encapsulates data. There is a huge literature about Object Oriented Design; an introduction to the theme is presented by Booch [4].

Different simulation applications can retrieve useful information from a Smart Object to accomplish a desired interaction task. The main idea is to provide a Smart Object with a maximum of information to attend different possible applications for the object. Each application will implement its *specific Smart Object reasoning* that will use only the applicable object features for its specific case.

The Smart Object approach introduces the following characteristics in an animation system:

- Decentralization of the animation control. By applying object and agent behaviors stored in a Smart Object, a lot of object-specific computation is released from the main animation control.
- Reusability of designed Smart Objects. A Smart Object can be modeled first for a specific application, and updated if needed for other applications without changing the usability of the original design.
- A simulation-based design is naturally achieved. The designer can take control of the loop: design, test and re-design. A designed Smart Object can be easily inserted into a simulation program, which gives feedback for improvements in the design.

Although the main focus here is to model interactions with virtual human agents, the presented Smart Object framework is also designed to be useful in interactions of other natures, as for example, 3D interactions using virtual reality devices.

In order to demonstrate some results of the proposed framework, two applications are described. One application reads simple text instructions to direct agents to interact with Smart Objects. The other application is a crowd simulation [14] in which interactions between some individual agents and Smart Objects are integrated.

The following sections are organized as follows: Section 2 gives an overview of concepts adapted from the Feature Modeling area. Section 3 describes in detail the Smart Object description and the graphical interface program used to model its features. Section 4 presents two applications using the Smart Object framework and section 5 concludes and presents some future work considerations.

2 Feature Modeling of Interactive Objects

Feature modeling is an expanding topic in the engineering field [16]. The word *feature* conjures up different ideas when presented to people from different backgrounds. A simple general definition, suitable for our purposes, is "a feature is a region of interest on the surface of a part" [20].

The main difficulty here is that, in trying to be general enough to cover all reasonable possibilities for a feature, such a definition fails to clarify things sufficiently to give a good mental picture.

From the engineering point of view, it is possible to classify features in three main areas: functional features, design features and manufacturing features [16]. As we progress from functional features through design features to manufacturing features, the quality of detail that must be supplied or deduced increases markedly. In the other hand, the utility of the feature definitions to the target application decreases. For example, manufacturing features of some piece may be hard to describe and have little importance while really using the piece. A similar compromise arises in the Smart Object case. This situation is depicted in figure 1 and will be explained later.

A huge literature is available for the feature modeling technique in the scope of engineering. A good coverage of the theme is done by Shah and Mantÿla [21].

In a Smart Object, we propose a new class of features that are interaction-features for simulation purposes. A more precise idea of a feature can be given as follows: all parts, movements and descriptions of an object that have some important role when interacting with an agent. For example, not only buttons, drawers and doors are considered as interaction features in an object, but also their movements and purposes.

As already mentioned, different interaction features are considered:

- Intrinsic object properties: properties that are part of the object design, for example: the movement description of its moving parts, physical properties such as weight and center of mass, and also a text description for identifying general objects purpose and the design intent.
- Interaction information: useful to aid an agent to perform each possible interaction with the object. For example: the position of some interaction part (like a knob or a button), specific hand interaction information (hand shape,

approach direction) and description of object movements that may control an agent (an escalator).

- Object behavior: an object can have various different behaviors, which may or may not be available, depending on the configuration of its state variables. For example, an automatic door can close only if some state variables are true: as one indicating that no agents are passing through the door, and another indicating that the door is open.
- Agent behaviors: associated with each object behavior, it is useful to have a description of some behavior that the agent should follow. For example, one possible behavior to model in an automatic door is to open itself when an agent comes nearby, give a feed point to the agent walk (in order to pass through the door), and then close.

Each application will implement its *specific Smart Object reasoning* that will make use only of the applicable object features for its specific case. For example, a virtual reality application in which the user wears a virtual glove to press a button to open a Smart Object door, will not make use of a proposed hand shape to press the button.

There is a trade-off when choosing which features to be considered in an application. As shown in figure 1, when taking into account the full set of object features, less reasoning computation is needed, but less realistic results are obtained. As an example, consider a door that has a behavior to control an agent passing through it. So, an application can easily control an agent passing through the door, by just using a supplied path. In this case, minimal computation is needed. But such solution would not be general in the sense that all agents would pass the door exactly in the same way. To reach more realistic results, external parameters should also take effect, as for example, the current agent emotional state [3].

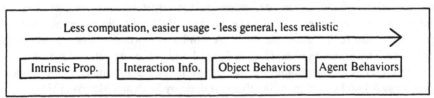

Fig. 1. Compromise between less computation vs. realism when choosing object features to use.

A complete Smart Object proposes a detailed solution for each possible interaction with the object. In each application, the specific reasoning program can decide whether to use the proposed solution or not. Doing so, the development of a specific reasoning is simplified by starting with following all proposed solutions, and then, gradually adjusting each solution to reach desired special cases.

The next section describes in detail how, and how far, the directives showed above are accomplished by the Smart Object.

3 The Smart Object Description

All the features of a Smart Object are described in a text-based script file. The geometry of the object is saved in any desired format being just referred from the script. This keeps the script file general enough to work in a variety of applications.

As most parameters in the script file are not easily defined in a text editor, a graphical interface program called *Smart Object Modeler* is used. The modeler is implemented using the Open Inventor library as graphical toolkit, and a simplified user interface layer over Motif.

3.1 Considered Features

The considered features in a Smart Object are identified in such a way as to give direct useful information for the many motion generators available in a human agent implementation. We have been designing and testing the Smart Object framework within the HUMANOID environment [6], and the AGENTlib motion control architecture [7]. The AGENTlib provides automatic management of action combination over an agent. For example, in such architecture, motion generators from an Inverse Kinematics module, and from a walking model [5], are easily combined and assigned to a given agent. The role of a Smart Object is to provide the needed parameters to correctly initialize each motion generator.

The Modeler is organized in different dialog boxes, according to the feature type being described. The organization of these dialogs has a direct relation with the script file organization. Each moveable part of an object has a separate geometry file. All parts are loaded according to a specified hierarchy, and they can be re-positioned. Figure 2 shows the two dialogs used to load and locate the parts of an automatic door. The positioning of each part can be done interactively using one of the six manipulators available in the Open Inventor. However, for precise alignments, it is also possible to explicitly edit each value of the final transformation matrix. Other intrinsic object properties such as physical attributes and text strings indicating semantic meaning object purpose are entered in another specific dialog.

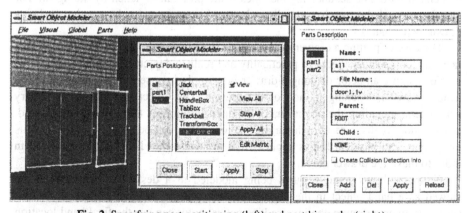

Fig. 2. Specifying part positioning (left) and part hierarchy (right).

Another intrinsic property is the definition of how each part of the object can move. Movements are called by *actions*, and are in fact, rotations or translations. To define an action, the same system of manipulators is used: the user selects some part of the object and presses the start button. The chosen manipulator will appear to let the user move the selected part. When the part moves to the desired final position, the user presses the stop button. The action is then calculated as the equivalent transformation matrix. Each action is independent of a part, so that the same defined movement can be used for different finalities.

The features described above constitute all considered intrinsic object features. Other features are used to define behaviors and interaction information: *positions* and *gestures*. A position is, in fact, a vector in space. Each position is identified by a name and can be later referenced from different behaviors. Figure 4 shows 3d vectors indicating key positions for the agent to reach for various Smart Objects.

A hand gesture-feature defines mainly an approach vector and a hand shape to aid agents to perform some dexterous activities, such as: grasping, button pressing, pulling a drawer, etc. Many gestures can be defined, and later referenced by their name in the behavior definitions.

Figure 3 shows the dialog used to define gestures. Each gesture can be located in space also by using manipulators. The hand shape of a gesture is defined by choosing one pre-defined hand posture file. Posture files can be updated using a dedicated interface program. Some pre-defined postures follow the classification given by Cutkosky [8]. This classification envisages grasping tasks, and hence, other postures such as button pressing, pulling and pushing are added.

Another parameter defined for a gesture is a joint configuration. A joint configuration supplies necessary parameters to the Inverse Kinematics motor, when the agent performs the gesture. Some parameters are joints to use (e.g., whether the arm alone or also some spinal joints) associated with weights to indicate which joint angles have more priority to move in relation to others.

A gesture has three flags that are applied in conjunction with an associated part. One indicates whether the gesture movement can be integrated with a grasping of the associated part. The second flag indicates if the part can be taken by the agent. The last flag says if the part has to follow the hand movement (such as a drawer being drawn by the hand).

The case of pulling a drawer exemplifies a situation where the reasoning algorithm faces the compromise between practicality and realism depicted in figure 1. A simple way of making an actor opening a drawer is to apply inverse kinematics to make the hand follow the opening motion of the drawer. The object provides all necessary parameters, including the action matrix to open the drawer that can be interpolated. But for more realistic results, the drawer action matrix can be used only to restrict its movement, and physical forces applied from the agents hand should be calculated in order to make the drawer move.

Figure 3 shows some gestures being modeled in a desk. Each gesture can be viewed as a hand object in the defined position and orientation. For example, in a gesture to open a drawer, the inverse kinematics motor can use the final hand location as end effector and the set of proposed joints to move. Another motion generator is concomitantly applied to interpolate the current hand shape to the final shape. After the hand position is reached, local geometric information can be used to perform subsequent movements, according to the gesture flags.

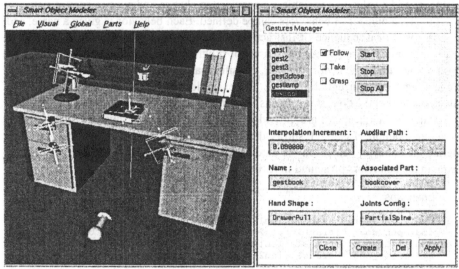

Fig. 3. Defining hand gestures (see Appendix).

Figure 4 shows three Smart Objects being modeled: an automatic door, a table with graspable fruits, and a door that opens after a button is pressed. In each case, some defined gestures and positions are shown.

The next subsection describes how the features modeled until now are referenced by behavior descriptions.

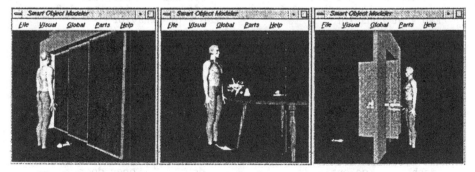

Fig. 4. Gestures and Positions being defined in different situations (see Appendix).

3.2 Behavior Features

To rule how the object will interact with an agent, three more types of features are used: commands, variable states, and behaviors.

A command is the full specification of some movement. It connects an action with an object part, and defines how the action is to be parameterized. Many commands can have the same identifying name, meaning that all should be performed in parallel.

Variables can be declared to define an object state. Instructions to check, set a value, or add a value to a variable are provided to change and query a current state.

Finally, a number of behaviors can be defined. Each behavior is given a name, and is composed of a sequence of instructions, called as *behavior items*. It is possible to view a behavior as a subroutine in a script program, where each behavior item is an instruction. Each behavior can be classified as either available or unavailable, depending on the current object state. For example, a behavior to open a door will be available only if the door state *open* is false, i. e., the door is closed.

Many behavior items are provided, and it is better to illustrate them with a concrete example. Listing 1 shows the commands, variables and behaviors used to define the behavior "enter" in the automatic door example. The following paragraphs explain the behaviors presented in listing 1.

```
COMMANDS
# name          action        part    ini    end    inc
cmd_open_door   translation1  part1   0.00   1.00   0.05
cmd_open_door   translation2  part2   0.00   1.00   0.05
cmd_close_door  translation1  part1   1.00   0.00   0.05
cmd_close_door  translation2  part2   1.00   0.00   0.05
END # of commands

VARIABLES
  open          0.0
  passing       0.0
END # of variables

BEHAVIOR go_out1                    BEHAVIOR go_out2
  Subroutine                          Subroutine
  addvar        passing  1.0          addvar        passing  1.0
  gotopos       pos_out1              gotopos       pos_out2
  addvar        passing -1.0          addvar        passing -1.0
END # of behavior                   END # of behavior

BEHAVIOR open_door                  BEHAVIOR close_door
  Subroutine                          Subroutine
  checkvar      open     0.0          checkvar      open     1.0
  changevar     open     1.0          checkvar      passing  0.0
  docmd         cmd_open_door         changevar     open     0.0
END                                   docmd         cmd_close_door
                                    END
BEHAVIOR enter1
  Subroutine                        BEHAVIOR enter2
  gotopos       pos_enter1            Subroutine
  dobh          open_door            gotopos       pos_enter2
  dobh          go_out1              dobh          open_door
  dobh          close_door           dobh          go_out2
END # of behavior                     dobh          close_door
                                    END # of behavior
BEHAVIOR enter
  Dobhifnear enter1 pos_enter1
  Dobhifnear enter2 pos_enter2
END # of behavior
```

Listing 1. Some behaviors used in the automatic door example.

The door was designed to correctly deal with many agents passing through it at the same time. So it has two state variables: *open*, indicating if the door is open or not, and *passing*, indicating how many agents are currently passing through it. All behaviors are declared as subroutines, which enforces them to be always unavailable. Only exception is behavior *enter* which is always available, as it does not have a *checkvar* item to test its availability.

When the application wants to control an agent entering the door, it searches for available behaviors in the Smart Object, and identifies the *enter* behavior as the desired one. This behavior simply calls another behavior, *enter1* or *enter2* depending whether the current agent position is near *pos_enter1*, or *pos_enter2* (pre-defined positions). This enables agents entering from any side of the door. Suppose that the behavior *enter1* is called. Then, each item of this behavior is carried out. The *gotopos* item gives a final position to the agent walk just before starting entering the door. At this point, if the door was not automatic, a gesture command *dogest* could be inserted to direct some specific agent action to open the door. Once the actor is ready to enter the door, three other behaviors are sequentially called: *open_door*, *go_out1*, and *close_door*.

The behavior *open_door* checks if the state variable *open* is false (zero), and if this is the case, the command to open the door is called and the state is changed. Note that the command *cmd_open_door* (similarly *cmd_close_door*) has two entries with the same name that makes the two parts of the door laterally translate at the same time. After the door is open, the behavior *go_out1* is called. This behavior updates the *passing* state variable value and supplies the position *pos_out1* to the agent to walk to the other side of the door. Finally, the behavior *close_door* is called. Then, the command to close the door is called if the variables *open* is true (one) and *passing* is zero, meaning that the door is open and no agents are currently walking trough the door. Only in that case, the door will then be closed.

It is difficult to define a closed and sufficient set of behavior items to use. Moreover, a complex script language to describe behaviors [19] is not the goal. The idea is to keep a simple script format with a direct interpretation to serve as guidance for reasoning algorithms, which any designer can create and test.

In the other hand, there are cases where a more complex functionality requires a complete programming language to be described. The functionality of a complete elevator (figure 8) is an example of how far the actual script language can go. To model more complex cases we intend to propose in the script language the possibility to call extern functions written in a C-like programming language. In this way, designers will still be able to model a basic functionality. Only some external functions will be provided by programmers in some specific cases. In section 4, other considerations about these objects are discussed.

Behavior definitions form an interface between stored objects features and the application-specific object reasoning. Figure 5 illustrates the connection between the modules. The simulation program requires a desired task to be performed. The reasoning module will then search for suitable available behaviors in the Smart Object. For any selected behavior, the reasoning module follows and executes each command of the behavior definition, retrieving the necessary data from the Smart Object.

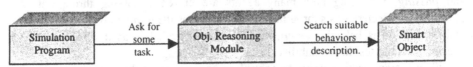

Fig. 5. Diagram showing the connection between the modules of a typical Smart Object application. Arrows represent function calls.

When a task to perform becomes more complex, it can be divided into smaller tasks. This work of dividing a task into sub-tasks can be done in the simulation program or in the reasoning module. In fact, the logical approach is to leave the reasoning module only to perform tasks that have a direct interpretation from the Smart Object behaviors. Then, additional layers of planning modules can be built according to the simulation program goal.

Another design choice must be made while modeling objects with too many potential interactions. In such cases, in order to exercise a greater control over the interactions, it is better to model a Smart Object for each part of the object, containing only basic behaviors. For example to model an agent interacting with a car, the car can be modeled as a combination of different Smart Objects: car door, radio, and the car panel. In this way, the simulation application can explicitly control a sequence of actions like: opening the car door, entering inside, turning on the radio, and starting the engine, thus permitting more personalized interactions. On the other hand, if the simulation program is concerned only with traffic simulation, the way an agent enters the car may not be important. In this case, a general behavior of entering the car can be encapsulated in the Smart Object.

In the current approach, object behaviors and agent behaviors are mixed in the same script language. In this way, whenever an agent starts an interaction, a process is created to interpret both agent and object behaviors. This approach is more direct to model, but for more complex objects, we intend to have one process always performing object behaviors, and whenever an agent starts an interaction, another process starts performing only agent behaviors. Processes can synchronize by checking global state variables.

3.3 Analysis of the Considered Features

By defining a general and complete set of behaviors, it is always possible to have a complete solution to perform a desired interaction.

By interpreting behavior definitions, the animation control is decentralized. Suppose the case of a complex simulation environment where many semantic rules are being processed all the time. One approach to direct such high level tasks is based on PaT-Nets [22]. In this case, when an agent is directed to go from one room to another, all local instructions on how to deal with encountered doors are stored inside each Smart Object door. This approach separates the high level planing from the specific low level Smart Object reasoning.

Another key characteristic is reusability. Reusability is reached in two levels. A first level is by using the same Smart Object in different applications. For this, different specific behaviors can be added and called when needed. Another level of reusability is achieved while designing a new Smart Object. In this case, the designer can merge any desired feature from some previously designed Smart Object.

It is also important to have the Smart Object specific reasoning easily connected with high level planners. This is possible by observing behavior names, and the object purpose description. This point is addressed in the next sub-section.

3.4 Connecting Behaviors to High Level Planners

There is a vast literature involving high level planners to guide an animation, and much of it focuses on connecting language to the animation, by interpreting and expanding given text instructions [1, 23, 10, 11]. In particular, Webber et al [23] identify the limited perception of agents as a main limitation to correctly interpret such text instructions, resulting in a poor knowledge construction. The proposed Smart Object framework can minimize this difficulty by providing in each Smart Object purpose-features that the agent can easily access to update its knowledge.

The Smart Object description provides different text statements that can be analyzed and used to update agents knowledge: text strings identifying behaviors, a semantic name, and general purposes description. For example, if a command like "Go out of the room" is given, the high level planner can map the action "go out" with a list of key names as "doors, windows, elevators, escalators". Then, it can search for the nearest Smart Object having one of these key names as its semantic name. Once the Smart Object is found, the next step is to choose the correct behavior by analyzing the names of each available behavior.

Section 4 presents some results obtained using a prototype of a system to control agents by giving simple text instructions based in the Smart Object behaviors.

4 Example of Smart Object Applications

Two applications have been developed using the Smart Object framework. One interprets simple text instructions to choose the closest Smart Object behavior to perform a desired task, and the other is a crowd simulation [14] that uses automatic doors and escalators as Smart Objects.

Figure 6 shows the layout of the application that interprets simple text instructions. It consists of a text entering area, a main graphical output window, and some auxiliary dialogs (as one describing available behaviors of a selected Smart Object). In the application, the user enters a command. If this is not recognized as a primitive command, the program looks into all Smart Objects in the scene to identify some text string.

In the example of figure 6, a simple command "close" can be given. After a string search, the program identifies the Smart Object having the closest available behavior, and executes it.

This application does not interpret natural language instructions, but makes a smart comparison of strings based on pre-designed strings contained in the Smart

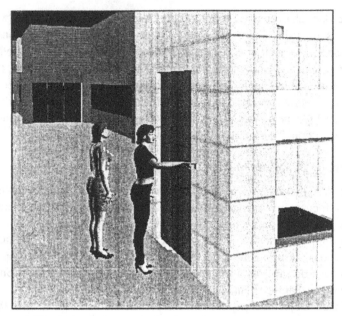

Fig. 8. Agents interacting with an elevator (see Appendix).

5 Conclusions and Future Work

This paper describes the Smart Object framework used to model general agent-object interactions. The approach used is based on a feature modeling of different kinds of interaction features, using a graphical interface program. This framework minimizes many difficulties encountered when using planning and object reasoning algorithms by achieving the following characteristics:

- Easy simulation-based design of Smart Objects.
- Easy reusability of Smart Objects to suit different applications.
- Decentralization of the animation control.
- Easy connection with high level planners.

Two applications using the proposed framework are described. These applications are still being developed and they use the same Smart Object reasoning algorithm. Many enhancements in this reasoning algorithm are being made, and this will certainly influence the creation of new interaction-features.

Both applications are being developed under the framework of AGENTlib [7] where it is also considered as an agent. A general reasoning system to interact object-agents with human-agents is being developed.

The main goal of the proposed framework is to be able to model the many agent-object interactions encountered in an urban environment simulation of a virtual city [9]. This implies connecting Smart Objects with a rule-based high-level planner, a crowd displacement simulation control, and environmental information.

Enhancements in the description of the object functionality are being done by including an optional and more powerful programming language, and by separating agent behaviors from object behaviors (see section 3.2). These improvements envisage also the usage of the Smart Object paradigm in applications of 3D interaction and manipulation of objects by real humans using virtual reality devices.

6 Acknowledgments

The authors are grateful to Dr. R. Boulic, P. Baerloch, S. R. Musse and Dr. S. Bandi for fruitful discussions, and to the anonymous referees for valuable suggestions. This research was supported by the Swiss National Foundation for Scientific Research and the Brazilian National Council for Scientific and Technologic Development (CNPq).

7 References

1. N. N. Badler, B. Webber, J. Kalita, and J. Esakov, "Animation from Instructions", In N. N. Badler, B. Barsky, and D. Zeltzer, eds, "Making Them Move: Mechanics, Control, and Animation of Articulated Figures", 51-93, Morgan-Kaufmann, 1990.

2. N. N. Badler, "Virtual Humans for Animation, Ergonomics, and Simulation", IEEE Workshop on Non-Rigid and Articulated Motion, Puerto Rico, June 97.

3. P. Bécheiraz and D. Thalmann, "A Model of Nonverbal Communication and Interpersonal Relationship Between Virtual Actors", Proceedings of Computer Animation'96, Geneva, 58-67, 1996.

4. G. Booch, "Object Oriented Design with Applications", The Benjamin Cummings Publishing Company, Inc., ISBN 0-8053-0091-0, 1991.

5. R. Boulic, N. Magnenat-Thalmann, and D. Thalmann, "A Global Human Walking Model with Real Time Kinematic Personification", The Visual Computer, 6, 344-358, 1990.

6. R. Boulic, T. Capin, Z. Huang, P. Kalra, B. Lintermann, N. Magnenat-Thalmann, L. Moccozet, T. Molet, I. Pandzic, K. Saar, A. Schmitt, J. Shen, and D. Thalmann. "The HUMANOID Environment for Interactive Animation of Multiple Deformable Human Characters", Proceedings of EUROGRAPHICS 95, Maastricht, The Netherlands, August 28 - September 1, 337-348, 1995.

7. R. Boulic, P. Becheiraz, L. Emering, and D. Thalmann, "Integration of Motion Control Techniques for Virtual Human and Avatar Real-Time Animation", In Proceedings of the VRST'97, 111-118, 1997.

8. M. R. Cutkosky, "On Grasp Choice, Grasp Models, and the Design of Hands for Manufacturing Tasks", IEEE Transactions on Robotics and Automation, Vol. 5, No. 3, 1989, 269-279.

9. N. Farenc, S. R. Musse, E. Schweiss, M. Kallmann, O. Aune, R. Boulic, and D. Thalmann, "One Step towards Virtual Human Management for Urban Environments Simulation", ECAI'98 Workshop of Intelligent Virtual Environments, 1998.

10. C. W. Geib, L. Levison, and M. B. Moore, "SodaJack: An Architecture for Agents that Search for and Manipulate Objects", Technical Report MS-CIS-94-13, University of Pennsylvania, 1994.

11. C. W. Geib, "The Intentional Planning System: ItPlanS", Proceedings of AIPS, 1994.

12. W. L. Johnson, and J. Rickel, "Steve: An Animated Pedagogical Agent for Procedural Training in Virtual Environments", Sigart Bulletin, ACM Press, vol. 8, number 1-4, 16-21, 1997.

13. L. Levison, "Connecting Planning and Acting via Object-Specific reasoning", PhD thesis, Dept. of Computer & Information Science, University of Pennsylvania, 1996.

14. S. R. Musse and D. Thalmann, "A Model of Human Crowd Behavior: Group Inter-Relationship and Collision Detection Analysis", EGCAS'97, Eurographics Workshop on Computer Animation and Simulation, 1997.

15. H. Noser, O. Renault, D. Thalmann, "Navigation for Digital Actors Based on Synthetic Vision, Memory, and Learning", Computer & Graphics, volume 19, number 1, 7-19, 1995.

16. S. Parry-Barwick, and A. Bowyer, "Is the Features Interface Ready?", In "Directions in Geometric Computing", Ed. Martin R., Information Geometers Ltd, UK, 1993, Cap. 4, 129-160.

17. A. Pentland, "Machine Understanding of Human Action", 7th International Forum on Frontier of Telecom Technology, 1995, Tokyo, Japan.

18. K. Russell, T. Starner, and A. Pentland, "Unencumbered Virtual Environments", International Joint Conference on Artificial Intelligence Entertainment and AI, ALife Workshop, 1995.

19. K. Perlin, and A. Goldberg, "Improv: A System for Scripting Interactive Actors in Virtual Worlds", Proceedings of SIGGRAPH'96, New Orleans, 205-216.

20. M. J. Pratt, and P. R. Wilson, "Requirements for Support of Form Features in a Solid Modeling System", Report R-85-ASPP-01, CAM-I, 1985.

21. J. J. Shah, and M. Mäntylä, "Parametric and Feature-Based CAD/CAM", John Wiley & Sons, inc. 1995, ISBN 0-471-00214-3.

22. B. Webber, and N. Badler, "Animation through Reactions, Transition Nets and Plans", Proceedings of the International Workshop on Human Interface Technology", Aizu, Japan, October, 1995.

23. B. Webber, N. N. Badler, B. Di Eugenio, C. Geib, L. Levison, and M. Moore, "Instructions, Intentions and Expectations", Artificial Intelligence Journal, 73, 253-269, 1995.

Assisted Articulation of Closed Polygonal Models

Marek Teichmann   Seth Teller

{marekt,seth}@graphics.lcs.mit.edu

Computer Graphics Group

Massachusetts Institute of Technology

Abstract

Creating articulated geometric models is a common task in animation systems. In some instances, models are procedurally instanced, and
articulated degrees of freedom are designed into the model. In other instances, the model is some geometric assemblage, and an articulated skeleton (sometimes called an "I-K skeleton") is bound to the model by the user,
typically by manual indication of a correspondence between elements of
each structure. In either case, some binding must be made to couple
boundary motions to those of the skeleton; this can be done for example
by generating spring networks or spatial deformation fields. Both processes can be tedious in the ordinary case, especially when the model to
be articulated is given only as a boundary representation, for example a
polygonal mesh representing a character's skin or clothing, or an object's
surface.

We present a simple method for assisted articulation of geometric models. Given a 3D polygonal mesh representing an object, an approximation
to the mesh's medial axis is efficiently computed using a 3D Voronoi diagram of the mesh vertices, and connectivity information within the mesh.
The medial axis is then simplified; the resulting tree structure has chains
of edges and nodes. We interpret selected nodes as joints of an I-K skeleton, and the chains connecting them as its links. A spring network is then
generated to bind the I-K skeleton to the object boundary, so that skeletal
motions will affect the boundary in a reasonable way, as specified by the
animator.

We show a user interface that allows interactive editing of the automatically constructed skeleton, and demonstrate the import, and mapping of
key-framed motion capture data to, a variety of initially static polygonal
objects.

Keywords: Animation, I-K skeleton, Medial axis, modeling, mesh deformation.

1 Introduction

Creating articulated geometric models is a common task in animation systems. In some instances, models are procedurally instanced, and articulated degrees of freedom are designed into the model. In other instances, the model is some geometric assemblage, and an articulated skeleton (sometimes called an "I-K skeleton") is bound to the model by the user, typically by manual indication of a correspondence between elements of each structure. In either case, some binding must be made to couple boundary motions to those of the skeleton; this can be done for example by generating spring networks or spatial deformation fields. Both processes can be tedious in the ordinary case, especially when the model to be articulated is given only as a boundary representation, for example a polygonal mesh representing a character's skin or clothing, or an object's surface.

The input to our system is a polygonal mesh of genus zero representing an object. We generate a tree-like skeleton with very little user intervention. We proceed in several steps. First, the medial axis of the object is approximated by a Voronoi skeleton. The user then selects a few points on the Voronoi skeleton to identify object features to be animated. The skeleton is then simplified by our algorithm to produce a tree, whose branches reach to the user selected points, and which otherwise lies well inside the object. This tree transformed into an I-K skeleton through user identified skeleton vertices, which become joints. The mesh is then automatically attached to the skeleton via a spring network. Subsequent user or keyframe-based manipulation of the skeleton results automatically in corresponding articulation of the original model.

2 Related Work

Springs and Bones. Koch et. al. [KGC+96] use data from CT and range scans to construct a bone structure, onto which they connect a skin mesh using a set of springs. Wilhelms and Van Gelder [WV97] use existing bone models, and a simple model of the underlying muscles to determine the changes in muscle shape. In both methods the skin is a triangular mesh with springs at edges, is connected via a spring network and is relatively close to the underlying simulated muscles or bone. The springs are generated by locating one (or several in [KGC+96]) points close to the mesh vertices on the underlying structure. In [WV97] a parameterization of the muscles is used to create such attachment points. In [LTW95], a scanned facial model is animated via a spring network which includes an estimated underlying skull, and a layer of springs representing simulated muscles. A method for more precise modeling of muscles connected to an anatomically correct skeleton has been shown in [SPCM97]. In [GTT89], finite element methods are used on a manually constructed structure for computing deformations of an articulated model.

Free Form Deformation. Free form deformation techniques are important techniques for animating meshes. They do however require some manually constructed underlying structure. Such an approach is described in [CHP89]. Recent examples include [MJ96], and [CR94]. For example, in [MJ96], a lattice around the part to be animated is required (see for example Figure 9 in [MJ96]). It is not clear how such a lattice would be constructed automatically, or be made consistent across an entire model. In this setting it appears difficult to assign intuitive animation variables.

Mesh editing. Techniques for multiresolution editing, as in [ZSS97] allow a user to manipulate meshes on a large or small scale. Here too however, it appears difficult to assign simple animation variables to the model in an automatic fashion.

Implicit surfaces. These have been used mainly for the animation of models constructed by hand. Recently, [SOP95] give a combined method for animating human figures, where rigid body transformations of a scanned polygonal mesh skin on a skeletal structure are combined with deformations based on implicit functions. This skeleton must however be constructed manually. For skeleton based implicit surface models, local deformations can be handled as described for example in [OCG97].

Skeleton construction. The problem of constructing a skeleton that is representative of an object is a well studied problem in pattern recognition, especially in two dimensions [OK95], and has also received some attention in graphics [FCGA97]. However, the notion of skeleton quality is domain dependent at present; there seems to be no algorithm that would always satisfy the subjective needs of an animator. In our method, we solicit a small amount of user input to solve this problem, and identify which parts of an object will be animated. It should also be noted that some of the methods above could be combined with the skeleton constructed by our method.

Contributions

This paper builds on a number of fundamental ideas from computational geometry and graph theory:

- The Voronoi diagram and medial axis of a set of polygons [Aur91, SPB95].

- Graph algorithms for computing the biconnected components of a graph [CLR90].

- An approximation algorithm for the medial axis of the model polygons, by the Voronoi diagram of a set of points on the surface of the objects [Hub96]. For dense meshes, this can be taken as the mesh vertices. For meshes with larger triangles, these are recursively subsampled.

- The notion of importance of a point on the medial axis: points with larger distance to the surface have greater importance [OK95], as do points selected by the user in our case.

This paper introduces several new techniques:

- Use of the Delaunay triangulation [Ede87] of mesh vertices *and* points inside the object. We use points of the Voronoi diagram to give a structure to the interior.

- An algorithm for reduction of the complex Voronoi skeleton to a simple tree given a small number of user selected Voronoi vertices designating the "tips" of object features to be animated.

- Automatic determination of a good attachment of a spring network to the reduced skeleton.

- A method for identifying which mesh vertices to attach by springs to each I-K skeleton branch, this is an important step for proper spring network behavior.

- A new type of "smart spring", whose constant changes according to local geometry.

3.1 Summary of our Method

We start with the approximation of the medial axis as mentioned above. The user selects a small number of "tips" to indicate which features of the model are to be imbued with articulation freedom. The skeleton is then automatically generated using a new graph reduction algorithm (see Section 4.2). The skeleton forming the medial axis approximation is viewed as a graph. The algorithm proceeds by identifying those vertices of the skeleton which can be removed without disconnecting the graph. Among those, only vertices of low importance (those close to the mesh surface) are removed. This process is repeated until a tree is obtained. Due to the selection of vertices to be removed, the tree lies near the "center" of the model, but is connected to the user selected tips.

The user can interactively add or remove points of articulation, as well as define local coordinate systems at each articulation. The system then connects these articulation points to animation variables, and provide a means to couple external animations (eg. keyframe data) to animate the model via the skeleton.

To connect the skin to the skeleton, we give an algorithm for creating spring network that allows the skin of the model to follow deformations of the skeleton, without breaks, folds or excessive stretching in the mesh for reasonable motions of the skeleton. We identify which mesh vertices are associated with each skeleton branch using the closest neighbors in a graph of mesh edges and mesh-skeleton Delaunay edges.

At animation time, for each animation frame, the spring network is simulated until it stabilizes, that is until a user specified threshold in the maximum displacement of mesh vertices is attained. The resulting mesh can be output for rendering.

We also allow interactive manipulation of the model by animating the skeleton manually, for example by exercising each joint. This is useful for tuning spring constants and deciding which degrees of freedom to add to or remove from the animation skeleton, and specifying local coordinate systems for easy attachment of external animation generators.

An important advantage of our technique with respect to anatomical modeling methods [WV97], is the low user interaction requirements. Our methods

allow model importation and skeleton construction after approximately 30 minutes of user interaction. Finding the I-K skeleton then takes a few minutes of unattended computation for a small model (5000 polygons). For larger models, this computation may take several hours, but need be done only once per model. After this step, the model is ready for animation. We give some running times in Section 6.

Our technique is model independent and requires no specific structure. It is mainly intended for models which have relatively long members, compared to the rest of the body, although we have successfully animated models like the Bunny.

In theory, our algorithm has a significant limitation: it works only for "closed" objects, that is, those that partition space into two components. Moreover, it works best for objects of genus zero (that is, those with the topology of a sphere). However, it often works well for more intricate objects, and we demonstrate that in practice it removes much of the burden of articulating imported objects. Another limitation, which might not be present for example in systems based on implicit surfaces, is that the range of motion resulting in a reasonable surface is limited by the spring network. In particular, full simulation of a non self-penetrating skin would require the addition of a collision detection and handling engine. Similar issues need to be handled by cloth simulations, see for example [CVT95].

In Section 4 we detail the skeleton construction steps. Some implementation details are given in Section 5, followed by a summary of results in Section 6. We conclude in Section 7.

4 Skeleton Construction

Our technique is based on approximating the medial axis of the mesh. There are a number of techniques for approximating the medial axis of a polyhedral object [SPB95]. The method we use is to sample the surface of the object and compute the Voronoi Diagram of the sample points [Hub96].

4.1 Medial Axis Approximation

Recall that the Medial axis of a surface is the set of points in space that are equidistant to two or more surface points. The Voronoi diagram of a set of point sites, divides space into a set of Voronoi regions. Each region corresponds to the set of points in space that are closest to the site associated with the region. The vertices of the regions, which we will use are equidistant to three (or more) sites.

The first step in the construction of the skeleton is to ensure the mesh is sufficiently dense, which is required for a good approximation of the medial axis. We add points on its surface recursively until a user specified inter-point distance maximum is met.

Next, we construct the Voronoi Diagram of the mesh vertices. For this purpose we compute the Delaunay triangulation of the mesh vertices. For each resulting tetrahedron, we compute the circumsphere of the tetrahedron, whose center point is a Voronoi vertex [Ede87]. Adjacency of Voronoi vertices is apparent; two Voronoi vertices are adjacent if their corresponding tetrahedra share a face. We thus obtain the skeleton of the Voronoi diagram of the mesh vertices.

This produces a number of points lying on the medial axis, in the interior and exterior of the object. This process takes $O(m^2)$ time in the worst case, where m is the number of mesh vertices, but we use an efficient randomized algorithm [CMS93] and this is not a bottleneck in our system. For example, for the Doll model with 20710 triangles (see Section 6), this process took 32 seconds. The next step is to eliminate those Voronoi vertices on the outside of the object. For each vertex point, this is accomplished by casting a ray from the point in an arbitrary direction and counting the number of intersections.

We use an alternate method in case the model contains more than one surface, but satisfies the property that triangles of each surface are properly oriented (say have outward oriented normals). We consider the triangle closest to the point and make sure the point is in the halfspace delimited by the plane of the triangle, and locally interior to the model, i.e. on the interior side of the triangle. If the model has no holes, this guarantees a correct answer. This technique also works well in practice if the surface has some small holes, as does the Bunny model: we use rays in several different directions to find a ray that intersects the mesh.

We thus obtain the portion of the skeleton of the Voronoi diagram lying on the inside of the object. In addition, with each vertex is associated the radius of the corresponding circumsphere, as constructed by the Delaunay triangulation. This radius approximates the distance from this point to the object surface. Finally, we delete Voronoi edges that traverse of the model boundary. (For models that have several parts, we cannot simply delete edges which intersect any triangle.)

4.2 Skeleton Specification

We next consider this skeleton as a graph and take advantage of metric distance information to simplify the skeleton. Intuitively, the goal is to obtain one branch corresponding to each of the object's members or salient features that the user wishes to animate, or wishes to remain in a fixed position. Since, as mentioned before, the definition of the skeleton is highly model and application dependent, we include a small amount of user input for its construction.

The user selects Voronoi vertices that are close to the "ends" of each branch or member of the model, such as for example at the tip of a finger. For example, in Figure 1, the user has selected the green vertices. These vertices will remain untouched by the algorithm, and will constitute the end points of each skeleton branch. This guarantees that each model member will be represented in the skeleton. Typically, for a humanoid model, the number of such points is less than 25. It is also possible to effect simple facial animation by choosing points near a mouth's center and corners, for example.

After this selection step, our skeleton simplification algorithm proceeds to automatically simplify the skeleton, as described below.

4.3 Skeleton Simplification

Our goal is to produce one chain of vertices per branch, in other words a tree, with the selected vertices as leaves. In addition, the skeleton should be as much in the center of the object as possible. We accomplish this as follows.

We consider the skeleton as an abstract graph, where the nodes are the vertices and the edges are the Voronoi edges. This graph is mostly connected. Occasionally, small stray connected components appear, and we take the largest connected component. We refer the reader to [CLR90] for definitions and algorithms related to graphs. We next iterate the following steps until the graph is a tree:

1. We compute the biconnected components of the current graph, initially the largest connected component, and identify the articulation points.

2. For each biconnected component we remove the vertex closest to the mesh surface (as indicated by the associated sphere radius). We ignore the articulation points of the graph, as removing these might cause the graph to become disconnected, and user specified vertices. We are thus guaranteed by the property of biconnected components that the graph remains connected.

We thus obtain a tree (assuming the user did not select three mutually adjacent vertices; an application of a Spanning Tree algorithm [CLR90] takes care of this problem). An example of a model with its associated skeleton can be seen in Figure 1.

The running time of one iteration above is $O(v + e)$, where v is the number of vertices, e the number of edges in the graph. The total time is therefore $O(v^2 + ve)$. In our case, v is the number of mesh and Voronoi vertices, which can be quite large for a complex mesh. For large models, we use a simplified version of the model generated with the algorithm of [SZL92].

The final step is a simplification of the resulting skeleton. Neighboring vertices that are closer than an interactively set user specified threshold are merged, producing a vertex at their midpoint. This threshold is weighted by the distance to the mesh to take into account mesh geometry.

4.4 Animation Skeleton Construction

At this point, the user is presented with a simple skeleton that is almost ready for manipulation. The user identifies selected skeleton vertices as articulation joints, optionally adjusting their position and splitting edges where desired. Each skeleton branch between user identified vertices becomes an animation skeleton branch. The user can also interactively orient the local coordinate system at each joint, for compatibility with keyframe or motion camera data from external animation systems.

We thus obtain the animation skeleton, where to each branch (shown in grey lines on the right in Figure 1) corresponds a chain of Voronoi vertices. The next step is to associate mesh vertices with each branch.

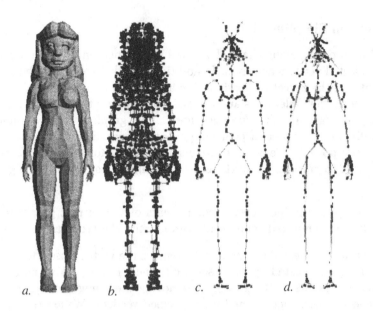

Figure 1: a. A woman model, b. The unsimplified skeleton, c. The simplified skeleton, d. with the I-K skeleton superposed.

4.5 Spring Network Construction

We now need to attach the mesh to the skeleton. We do this by constructing a spring network. The network consists of springs at the mesh edges, and springs connecting mesh vertices to the skeleton vertices. The difficulty lies in finding the latter edges. We accomplish this by computing the three dimensional Delaunay triangulation of the points consisting of both the mesh vertices and the skeleton vertices. See Figure 2 for an example. The edges, deleted in Figure 2.b, have been identified as lying on the outside of the model. The Delaunay triangulation algorithm returns a set of tetrahedra triangulating the convex hull of all the mesh and skeleton points. This step takes $O((m + s)^2)$ time in the worst case, where m is the number of mesh vertices, s the number of skeleton vertices, which is usually small. As in the Voronoi diagram computation, it is fairly efficient in practice, and required 45 seconds for the Doll model.

We take the edges of the tetrahedra and delete all edges that connect a skeleton vertex to a skeleton vertex, and all edges between mesh vertices, except those that correspond to edges in the triangulated mesh. This however occasionally causes small isolated regions of orphan mesh vertices. This occurs when in the original Delaunay triangulation, those vertices were closer to each other than to the skeleton. When the spring network is animated, this would cause that section of the mesh to lose its shape. We simply connect each orphan vertex to the skeleton vertex of closest link distance in the graph.

4.6 Spring Network Animation

Finally, each mesh vertex is associated with the closest skeleton vertex, and hence to one animation skeleton branch. This is important for the animation, see below. The skeleton construction is now complete; thereafter, the spring network simulation runs continuously thereafter.

When the user, or an external animation engine, rotates a specific branch of the animation skeleton, we move the mesh vertices associated with the entire skeleton sub-branch being moved, by the same rotation. The skeleton geometry itself however is maintained using standard hierarchical instancing. This method provides a good starting point for the spring network, which achieves stability faster than if we were to rely on the springs alone to find the new mesh vertex positions. In addition, for mesh vertices connected to both a non-rotated and a rotated skeleton section, we use a weighted average of the previous and new positions respectively. The weights are determined according to the number of springs connecting the vertex to each branch.

The spring constants are selected in a way similar to that in [WV97]. Our main contribution here is the introduction of "smart springs", to improve handing of cases where the mesh folds on itself during large motions. In [WV97], the problem is solved by shortening the spring rest length on the springs corresponding to the the mesh edges, and reducing the constant when these springs are compressed. We in addition determine if the mesh has been folded on itself by maintaining the normals of the triangles adjacent to each vertex. If this occurs, the spring constants of the springs attached between the affected vertices are substantially reduced, and the spring lengths are temporarily reduced (until stretched again).

Figure 2d. shows the spring network in action. The grey levels in the triangle edges indicate the current local "temperature" of the spring network relative to the current maximum. This represents the amount of change each vertex is undergoing due to the network simulation at the moment the image was recorded. Note that, even after a large motion, the majority of points on a branch that was moved remain motionless with respect to the branch; only near the joint do the vertices undergo large changes.

Our system also provides means to do key-frame animation: either via user specified positions, or externally input positions. We can save a model at each frame for later rendering after the spring network has stabilized. In Figure 3 we show several models in varying poses.

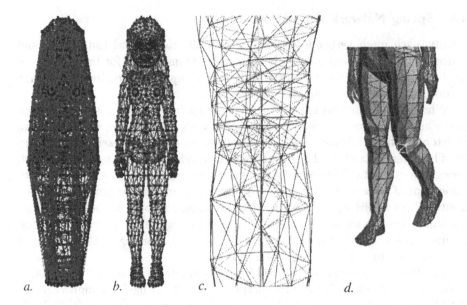

Figure 2: a. The initial Delaunay triangulation. b. After removal of external edges. c. Leg detail. d. The mesh is automatically readjusted when the knee is bent.

5 Implementation Details

The Delaunay triangulation computations are done using the robust HULL package of Clarkson [Cla], which implements a randomized incremental construction algorithm [CMS93]. This package computes the convex hull of a set of points in any (small) dimension, which by well known transformations can be used for finding the Delaunay triangulation, or as outlined above, the Voronoi diagram of a set of points.

This code returns a list of simplices triangulating the input points. We use the LEDA [MN95] graph data type to store and manipulate the result. For the Delaunay triangulation, we insert the input points as nodes in the graph, along with their position and other bookkeeping information. Tetrahedral edges become graph edges.

For the Voronoi diagram, the centers of the tetrahedra are used as graph nodes. A graph edge corresponds to each tetrahedral face not on the convex hull of the entire set of points.

6 Results

We have imported and created skeletons for a number of models, from small (thousand polygon models), to complex (thirty thousand) polygon models. Our system has no inherent limits on model size. For efficiency however, skeleton creation for larger models is best done by prior simplification of the model. The full resolution model can then be used for animation.

Our models include one (the Doll) which is partially articulated, and contains polygons in their interior. This did not affect the functionality of the spring network. We show the original models and some resulting poses in Figure 3.

In the table below, we give our model sizes in the number of triangles, the number of initial Voronoi vertices before reduction (labeled Voronoi), the number of springs, and skeleton creation times.

Model	Size	Voronoi	Springs	Unattended processing time
Doll	5944	9938	36260	13.2 minutes
Bunny	16301	27539	35040	34.5 minutes
Woman	20710	72371	127407	4 hours
Man	29266	46565	181001	6 hours

The computation of the Voronoi diagram and the Delaunay triangulation did not exceed 1 minute for any of the models listed. The number of Voronoi vertices forming the skeleton is, after simplification, on the order of 200 to 500 for all models, and is user adjustable. For smaller models (10000 triangles), the spring network stabilizes in under 3 seconds. In addition, since the portion of the model attached to only the portion of the skeleton that is rotated is first rigidly rotated before spring simulation is run, the general shape of the model is immediately apparent. For the larger models, depending on the size of the motion, and the value of a "drag" coefficient in our spring simulation, it can take up to 10 seconds for the larger models.

7 Discussion and Concluding Remarks

We have presented a useful tool for animators, which should simplify considerably the process of embedding animation controls into existing boundary models.

An advantage of our method over anatomical modeling methods such as [WV97] is the absence of a requirement for detailed structure below the skin, thus avoiding the need for the manual construction of such a structure. While such a structure allows the modeling of a "muscle bulge" effect, our method is particularly appropriate for models requiring no such effects, although such extensions can be easily imagined.

Improvements to our methods are possible. The skeleton simplification algorithm, while guaranteed to produce a tree, can take considerable time on large models. We deal with this problem by using an existing simplification algorithm, but it would be interesting to find a faster one. It would seem for example, that it would be desirable to delete more than one vertex per biconnected component; however this is in general not possible, as in, for example, when the component is formed by one cycle. Collision detection with scene objects, and self-collision detection would allow the simulation of interactions of the model with its environment. Finally, an easy extension is to place sampled cylinders around skeleton edges, tapered toward the ends, to improve control of skin when skeleton edges are twisted.

Figure 3: Three models and a pose obtained during animation. The originals are on the left, their skeletons on the right.

Finally, it would be interesting to combine our methods with multiresolution representations, as in [Hop96].

Acknowledgments

We would like to thank Viewpoint Data Labs for their generosity in providing many of the models for our work, and the Stanford Data Repository for making their models available.

References

[Aur91]   F. Aurenhammer. Voronoi diagrams: A survey of a fundamental geometric data structure. *ACM Comput. Surv.*, 23:345–405, 1991.

[CHP89]   John E. Chadwick, David R. Haumann, and Richard E. Parent. Layered construction for deformable animated characters. In Jeffrey Lane, editor, *Computer Graphics (SIGGRAPH '89 Proceedings)*, volume 23, pages 243–252, July 1989.

[Cla]   H. Clarkson. *Hull*. Convex hull library, http://cm.bell-labs.com/netlib/voronoi/hull.html.

[CLR90]   T. H. Cormen, C. E. Leiserson, and R. L. Rivest. *Introduction to Algorithms*. MIT Press, Cambridge, MA, 1990.

[CMS93]   K. L. Clarkson, K. Mehlhorn, and R. Seidel. Four results on randomized incremental constructions. *Comput. Geom. Theory Appl.*, 3(4):185–212, 1993.

[CR94]   Yu–Kuang Chang and Alyn P. Rockwood. A generalized de Casteljau approach to 3D free–Form deformation. In Andrew Glassner, editor, *Proceedings of SIGGRAPH '94 (Orlando, Florida, July 24–29, 1994)*, Computer Graphics Proceedings, Annual Conference Series, pages 257–260. ACM SIGGRAPH, ACM Press, July 1994.

[CVT95]   Martin Courshesnes, Pascal Volino, and Nadia Magnenat Thalmann. Versatile and efficient techniques for simulating cloth and other deformable objects. In Robert Cook, editor, *SIGGRAPH 95 Conference Proceedings*, Annual Conference Series, pages 137–144. ACM SIGGRAPH, Addison Wesley, August 1995. held in Los Angeles, California, 06-11 August 1995.

[Ede87]   H. Edelsbrunner. *Algorithms in Combinatorial Geometry*, volume 10 of *EATCS Monographs on Theoretical Computer Science*. Springer-Verlag, Heidelberg, West Germany, 1987.

[FCGA97]   Eric Ferley, Marie-Paule Cani-Gascuel, and Dominique Attali. Skeletal reconstruction of branching shapes. *Computer Graphics Forum*, 16(5), December 1997.

[GTT89]   Jean-Paul Gourret, Nadia Magnenat Thalmann, and Daniel Thalmann. Simulation of object and human skin deformations in a grasping task. In Jeffrey Lane, editor, *Computer Graphics (SIGGRAPH '89 Proceedings)*, volume 23, pages 21–30, July 1989.

[Hop96]   Hugues Hoppe. Progressive meshes. In Holly Rushmeier, editor, *SIGGRAPH 96 Conference Proceedings*, Annual Conference Series, pages 99–108. ACM SIGGRAPH, Addison Wesley, August 1996. held in New Orleans, Louisiana, 04-09 August 1996.

[Hub96]   P. M. Hubbard. Approximating polyhedra with spheres for time-critical collision detection. *ACM Transactions on Graphics*, 15(3):179–210, 1996.

[KGC+96]   R. M. Koch, M. H. Gross, F. R. Carls, D. F. von Büren, G. Fankhauser, and Y. Parish. Simulating facial surgery using finite element methods. In Holly Rushmeier, editor, *SIGGRAPH 96 Conference Proceedings*, Annual Conference Series, pages 421–428. ACM SIGGRAPH, Addison Wesley, August 1996. held in New Orleans, Louisiana, 04-09 August 1996.

[LTW95]   Yuencheng Lee, Demetri Terzopoulos, and Keith Waters. Realistic face modeling for animation. In Robert Cook, editor, *SIGGRAPH 95 Conference Proceedings*, Annual Conference Series, pages 55–62. ACM SIGGRAPH, Addison Wesley, August 1995. held in Los Angeles, California, 06-11 August 1995.

[MJ96]   Ron MacCracken and Kenneth I. Joy. Free-Form deformations with lattices of arbitrary topology. In Holly Rushmeier, editor, *SIGGRAPH 96 Conference Proceedings*, Annual Conference Series, pages 181–188. ACM SIGGRAPH, Addison Wesley, August 1996. held in New Orleans, Louisiana, 04-09 August 1996.

[MN95]   K. Mehlhorn and S. Näher. LEDA: a platform for combinatorial and geometric computing. *Commun. ACM*, 38:96–102, 1995.

[OCG97]   Agata Opalach and Marie-Paule Cani-Gascuel. Local deformations for animation of implicit surfaces. In *SCCG'97*, Bratislava, Slovakia, 1997.

[OK95]   R.L. Ogniewicz and O. Kübler. Hierarchic voronoi skeletons. *Pattern Recognition*, 28(3):343–359, 1995.

[SOP95]   K. Singh, J. Ohya, and R. Parent. Human figures synthesis and animation for virtual space teleconferencing. *IEEE VRAIS*, pages 118–125, 1995.

[SPB95]   E.C. Sherbrooke, N.M. Patrikalakis, and E. Brisson. An algorithm for the medial axis transform of 3d polyhedral solids. In *Proc. ACM Siggraph Sympos. Solid Modeling*, pages 187–199, 1995.

[SPCM97]   F. Scheepers, R.E. Parent, W.E. Carlson, and S.F. May. Anatomy-based modeling of the human musculature. In *Computer Graphics (SIGGRAPH '97 Proceedings)*, pages 163–172, July 1997.

[SZL92]   William J. Schroeder, Jonathan A. Zarge, and William E. Lorensen. Decimation of triangle meshes. In Edwin E. Catmull, editor, *Com-*

puter Graphics (SIGGRAPH '92 Proceedings), volume 26, pages 65–70, July 1992.

[WV97]   Jane Wilhelms and Allen Van Gelder. Anatomically based modeling. In Turner Whitted, editor, *SIGGRAPH 97 Conference Proceedings*, Annual Conference Series, pages 173–180. ACM SIGGRAPH, Addison Wesley, August 1997.

[ZSS97]   Denis Zorin, Peter Schröder, and Wim Sweldens. Interactive multiresolution mesh editing. In Turner Whitted, editor, *SIGGRAPH 97 Conference Proceedings*, Annual Conference Series, pages 259–268. ACM SIGGRAPH, Addison Wesley, August 1997.

STIGMA: a 4-dimensional modeller for animation

Sylvain Brandel, Dominique Bechmann, Yves Bertrand

LSIIT UPRES-A ULP-CNRS 7005 - Université Louis-Pasteur
Pôle API - boulevard Sébastien Brant - F-67400 ILLKIRCH Cedex
e-mail : {brandel,bechmann,bertrand}@dpt-info.u-strasbg.fr

Abstract

This article presents an animation method and a software based on 4-D object modelling. This method uses a topological model and a free-form deformation model. It defines a set of 4-D modelling operations for the construction of 4-D objects. The resulting animation is a sequence of 3-D objects, obtained by successive sections of 4-D object. Using 4-D objects allows topological modification of the animated 3-D objects, such as the merging and the splitting of volumes.

1 Introduction

A great number of works have shown that geometric modelling, deformations and animation are three closely connected fields. 3-D deformations are powerful tools of 3-D modelling, as are the FFD for instance [19], extended to 3-D animation [9]. The n-D deformation model $DOGME$ [3] can be used in 4-D to generate 3-D animations [4] [6]. Some animation models are based on creating 3-D objects and describing the behaviour of this object over time [9] [12] [17] [18]. Alternatively, an other method consists in creating and deforming 4-D objects by identifying the time component with the three spatial components [4] [6]. However, a common restriction of these methods is that the topology of the objects is never modified. In the general public, the software offer many advanced operations, but without topological modifications.

One animation method [1] allows topological modifications. It consists in creating a 4-D object by the extrusion of a 3-D object, then applying a 4-D deformation, and then cutting this 4-D object by a hyperplane. Another method to build 4-D objects consists in computing the cartesian product of two objects [10]. This operation is the generalization of the extrusion operation. The type of the resulting animation depends on the type of the operations used to create the 4-D objects. For instance, the extrusion of a 3-D sphere is inevitably a 4-D sphere. In the section of this 4-D sphere, a 3-D object can be split into several 3-D objects, but these objects cannot be merged into a single object. Only toric objects allow these types of deformations.

In order to allow these animations, and all other types of animations, it is necessary to use a large set of operations. These operations allow to model 4-D objects with any shape and any topological structure. In this way, we design and implemant a geometric modeller of 4-D objects, $STIGMA$, who proposes such a set of operations. In this paper, we present the bases of this modeller's design.

We begin in section 2 by precisely explaining the "4-D" term, and the types of the operations detailed in the next sections. Section 3 describes the topological model used by $STIGMA$. Section 4 discusses the visualization problem and the underlying topological operations. And before concluding, we present in section 5 all the possible types of operations.

2   4-D modelling

$STIGMA$ is built on a topology-based model of geometric objects. On the one hand, a topological model represents the structure of objects, who are organized in a finite number of cells (vertices, edges, faces, etc.). On the other hand, an embedding model is used, to define the shape of these cells.

In classical boundary representation (B-rep), a 3-D object is represented by its boundary, i.e. by a 2-D manifold. In combinatorial representation, this manifold is subdivided in a finite number of vertices, edges and faces. This 2-D object is embedded in a 3-D space which contains the initial object. For instance, we use a 2-D B-rep model and we associate 3-D points with the vertices of the model, in order to represent polyhedral surfaces. In this case, these models are winged-edge structure [2] [21], the 2-maps [13] and the 2-G-maps [15].

More generally, other models based on topology allow to represent topologically 3-D objects, such as the subdivision of the subsoil in geological layers. These models are, for instance, the radial-edge structure [22], the 3-maps [16] and the 3-G-maps [11] [15]. These models also allow to represent the development of objects as plants or animals [20].

Keeping the B-rep point of view, an n-D object is represented by its boundary, which is an $(n-1)$-object. In this case, a topologically 3-D object can be embedded in a 4-D space, in order to represent the boundary of the 4-D object. In this way, a 3-D topological model could be a 3-G-map, whose vertices are embedded in 4-D points [1]. The extrusion of a 2-G-map provides a 3-G-map. Applying the deformation model $DOGME$ [3] on 4-D points determines the shape of the 3-G-map. The fourth dimension of the 4-D points represents time. Figure 1.a shows a grid extruded along a straight polygonal line. Figure 1.b shows a construction that is topologically identical to the one in figure 1.a. But in figure 1.b, $DOGME$ controls the shape of the extruded object and the shape of the resulting sections. Figure 2.a shows a cube (a 2-G-map), who is extruded, yielding a hypercube, represented by a translation (figure 2.b) and by a scaling operation (figure 2.c). Figure 3.a shows the six faces of the 3-D cube of figure 2.a, and figure 3.b shows the eight volumes of the hypercube of figures 2.b and 2.c. The intersection between a cutting hyperplane and a 3-G-map embedded in 4-D is a 2-G-map embedded in 3-D, i.e. a 3-D object in boundary representation. The succession of these sections presents a succession of not necessarily connected 3-D objects and represents a 3-D animation.

Since this type of animation is built only with a privileged operation, our goal here

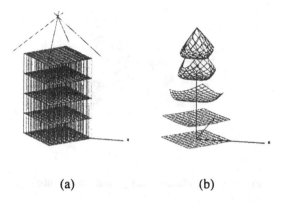

(a)   (b)

Figure 1: Extrusion (b) of a planar 2-G-map (a).

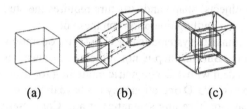

(a)   (b)   (c)

Figure 2: The extrusion of a cube (a): 2 representations (b and c).

is to design a general 4-D modeller with numerous operations. This is why we propose to distinguish four types of operations:

- the 3-D modelling operations, transforming one or more 3-D objects into one or more 3-D objects (section 5.1),

- the 4-D modelling operations, transforming one or more 4-D objects into one or more 4-D objects (section 5.3),

- the operations increasing the number of dimensions, transforming 3-D objects into 4-D objects: an example of this type of operation is the extrusion (section 5.2),

- the operations decreasing the number of dimensions, transforming 4-D objects into 3-D objects: an example of this type of operation is the section by a hyper-plane (section 4).

Studying those operations allows first to *extend the field of the possible animations*. More particularly, we want to obtain an animation with any number of splittings and mergings, in any order. This study allows *to improve the control of the shape and the structure of the* $4 - D$ *objects*. In fact, given a 4-D object and a cutting hyper-plane, the associated animation is difficultly predictable. To have an efficient control

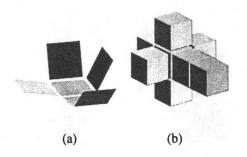

(a)   (b)

Figure 3: An unfolded cube (a) and a hypercube (b).

of the animation, it is essential to have a precise control of the structure and shape of the initial 4-D object. Extending the set of possible animations and achieving accurate control over the 4-D objects' shape and structure requires the study and the design of the most complete set of handling operations on these objects.

A first step is to translate systematically in 4-D the operations of the classical 3-. D geometric modelling. But this step is not sufficient, because our goal is to produce animations, and not to deal with 4-D geometric modelling for its own sake. This means that the 4-D counterpart of a 3-D operation may not have the same semantics as the 3-D operation itself or may not have any semantics at all. Conversely, there may be 4-D modelling operations for animation without any relevant semantics in 3-D geometric modelling.

Section 3 presents the G-maps. Section 4 details the problems about the manipulaton and the visualization of the 4-D objects. The operation decreasing the number of dimensions is also explained. In fact, this operation proposes different methods to project a 4-D object in 3-D, and solves a few visualization problems. Section 5 presents the three other types of operations.

3 Topological model

3.1 Generalized maps

Generalized maps are the topological model used in $STIGMA$. Using a single model allows to develop a homogeonous and robust modeller. It is true that some objects, such as orientables objects, could be represented more easily with other models. On the other hand the non-manifold cannot be represented with the generalized maps.

This section recalls the definition of the 3 dimensional generalized maps, called 3-G-maps. We do this by decomposing a simple geometric object (see figure 4) into its cells. The object in figure 4 is a pyramid on the top of a cube. On figure 5.a, we disconnect both volumes. Let P be the bottom face of the pyramid, and C the top face of the cube. On figure 5.a, the adjacent relations between P and C are shown by a thick line. The faces are disconnected on figure 5.b, the edges are disconnected on figure 5.c, and the vertices disconnected on figure 5.d. The adjacent relations between the faces (figure 5.b), between the edges (figure 5.c) and between the vertices (figure 5.d) are shown by thick lines. These vertices, called *darts*, are the unique kind of element of the of G-maps' definition.

Figure 4: Cube and pyramid.

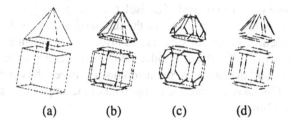

(a)	(b)	(c)	(d)

Figure 5: Disconnection of volumes (a), faces (b), edges (c) and vertices (d).

Each face P or C is made of eight darts (see figure 5.d). Each dart of P matches with one of C. Now, we replace the adjacence relation between the volumes (figure 5.a) by a symmetrical relation who associates a dart of P with the corresponding dart of C. Let α_3 be this relation. α_3 is represented by thick lines on figure 6.a. α_3 allows to "extend" the adjacence relation between the volumes to each dart. In the same way, we replace the adjacence relation between faces (figure 5.b) by a relation between darts, called α_2 (figure 6.b). The adjacence relation between faces has been extended to the faces' darts. In the same way, the adjacence relation between edges (figure 5.c) is extended to a relation between darts, called α_1 (figure 6.c). The relation between vertices, called α_0, is already a relation between the darts, so no extension is necessary.

The 3 *dimensional generalized map* (figure 6.d) represents the topology of the object on figure 4. This 3-G-map is the algebra $G = (B, \alpha_0, \alpha_1, \alpha_2, \alpha_3)$, where B is the set of darts obtained by the decomposition of the object.

3.2 Cells of generalized maps

We have to define the cells of the topological model in a G-map. These cells are often used to define the shape of objects, expressed in terms of points, curves, surfaces, etc. Moreover, some algorithms must identify these cells.

This is done by isolating all of the parts of the 3-G-map corresponding to a cell. We isolate the vertices, i.e. the 0-cells, by suppressing the α_0 relation. The suppression of α_0 on the 3-G-map represented on figure 6.d produces the 2-G-map represented on

108

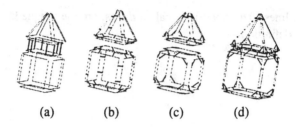

(a) (b) (c) (d)

Figure 6: Extension of the relations between volumes (a), faces (b) and edges (c), and the 3-G-map (d).

figure 7.a. Each connected component of this 2-G-map represents one of the object's vertices. In the same way, the removal of α_1 isolates the edges (figure 7.b), the suppression of α_2 isolates the faces (figure 7.c), and the suppression of α_3 isolates the volumes (figure 7.d). In practice, we do not suppress an involution to obtain a cell, we simply ignore it during the traversals. If we consider the G-map as a graph, the vertices of this graph are the darts, and the edges are the involutions between the darts. A connected component of the G-map is a connected component of the graph. This property allows to define the cells' G-maps.

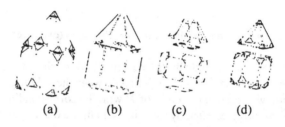

(a) (b) (c) (d)

Figure 7: Vertices (a), Edges (b), faces (c) and volumes (d) of the 3-G-map.

3.3 Embedding of the generalized maps

In the development of $STIGMA$, we reduce the embedding of the generalized maps to the embedding of the vertices. In this way, we associate a point with four co-ordinates to each connected component of the G-map of figure 7.a. The fourth dimension of these points represents time.

4 Visualization of 4-D objects

4.1 Visualization problems

All of the C.A.D. software display 3-D objects with a perspective effect. They also generally use the projection of these objects on the three orthtropic planes. This is because before C.A.D. was commonly used, all design tools such as the drawing board were 2-D tools. In C.A.D. software, we can use 2-D design with a great number of 2-D tools, in order to work on the projections of the 3-D objects. More fundamentally, we can decompose numerous complex 3-D objects into a set of simple 3-D objects, i.e. 3-D objects achieved by the extrusion of 2-D objects for instance. In an n-D space, visualizing and manipulating the internal structures of an n-D object is a difficult task. In the same n-D space, manipuleting an $(n-1)$-D object is easier, because we have the n-th dimension at our disposal. This is the reason why the B-rep model is so commonly used. In B-rep, in a 3-D space, we manipulate the boundary of the objects which is a topologically 2-D object.

In Classical 3-D modelling, the internal structure of the manipulated objects is often simple. In the case of the B-rep, the objects have no internal structure. Moreover, there are no intersections between the different volumes of the objects. There are only intersections along the common faces.

In $STIGMA$, we manipulate 4-D objects, and their boundaries are 3-D objects. This 3-D boundary has numerous internal structures. The more these structures are complex, the more the resulting animations are rich. These objects are embedded in 4-D then projected in 3-D. Numerous self-intersections appear during the projection, such as self-intersections between the faces of a 3-D object on a screen.

This is why we have more visualization problems in 4-D modelling than in 3-D modelling. In 3-D modelling, visualization and manipulation are made easier thanks to 2-D projections. In 4-D, there are several possible ways to project and extract 3-D information from the 4-D objects. In a first method, we simply project the 4-D object on a hyperplane. In an other method, the 4-D object is completely displayed, and the display mode depends on the part of the object which is being displayed. The last method displays the sections of the 4-D object by a cutting hyperplane. Some classical operations of B-rep modelling are used for the visualization of 4-D objects. These operations comprise boundary calculus, cell-fusion, closure.

4.2   The forgetting of a co-ordinate

Forgetting a co-ordinate consists in considering only three co-ordinates for each of the objects' points (whatever the value of the fourth co-ordinate). That amounts to projecting the object in one of the four hyperplanes xyz, xyt, xzt or yzt. The first hyperplane allows to project the 4-D object along the time axis, or display 4-D objects in which all of the time compenents are identical.

Figure 8.a shows a little robot in which all time components are zero. It is represented as it may have been represented in 3-D. Figures 8.b, 8.c and 8.d show the projections of this robot in xyt, xzt and yzt subspaces.

Figure 9.a presents a geological object called salt dome. In the subsoil, geological layers have different densities. The density of a salt layer is lower than the density of the layers above. This salt layer is deformed and in turn deforms the layers above before piercing them. Figures 9.b, 9.c and 9.d present the three projections of this object.

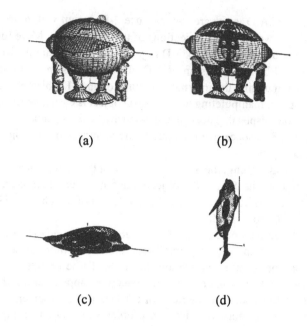

(a)

(b)

(c)

(d)

Figure 8: A robot projected in the subspaces xyz (a), xyt (b), xzt (c) and yzt (d).

4.3 Complete visualization

The 4-D objects can also be incompletely displayed, without any projection. Figure 2 shows the complete visualization of a hypercube. Figure 10.a shows a hypersphere resulting from the extrusion of a sphere along a polygonal line with three segments. Figure 10.b shows the same hypersphere obtained with a scaling operation. For a clearer representation of the inner structure of the objects, all of the faces which connect points with the same date are displayed with wire frames where as the faces which connect points with different dates are displayed with solid surfaces. In this way, on figure 10.a, we "show" in the solid surface mode four 3-D spheres, who are the four key-points of the extrusion-line.

However, from the topological point of view, the parts of the 4-D object displayed with solid surfaces are not really 3-D spheres. In order to understand the reason, figure 11 presents a 2-D example. Figure 11.a shows a chevron and an extrusion-line with two segments. Figure 11.b shows the extrusion of the chevron along the line. The edges connecting two dates are displayed with fine lines, and the edges who connect two points in a same date are displayed in thick lines. Visually, the three pairs of edges in thick lines look like three chevrons, corresponding to the three key-points of the extrusion-line. Figure 11.c presents the corresponding G-map, with three "impressions" of the initial chevron, but this chevron does not really exist in the G-map.

Now, we want to visualize three chevrons in the object of figure 11. In order to really obtain the three chevrons, we have to merge all pairs of faces who are incident at a same edge in fine line. By this same way, in the object of figure 10, we want to

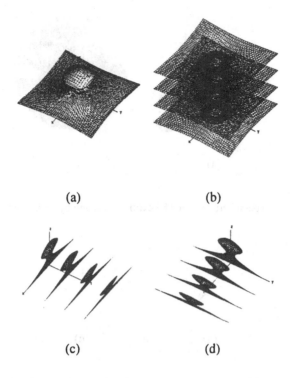

(a)   (b)

(c)   (d)

Figure 9: Four projections of a diapir.

obtain four 3-D spheres. To do this, we have to merge all pairs of volumes incident at
a same face in fine line. Figure 12.a presents an instance with two quadrileterals and
the fusion of the faces. This operation exactly corresponds to an Euler-operator, called
kef (kill-edge-face). Figure 12.b shows the 3-D equivalent operation with two cubes
and the fusion of volumes. This operation corresponds to the kfl (kill-face-loop) and
$kflrs$ (kill-face-loop-region-shell) operators [22]. The fusion of faces is applied to the
objects of figure 11.b (figure 13.a), and the fusion of volumes is applied to the object of
figure 10.a (figure 13.b).

In a 4-D object obtained by extrusion, if we apply the fusion-operation at the faces
who connect two dates, we can visualize the key-points of the corresponding 3-D animation. This operation can also be applied at the faces who have all their points in a
same date. Figure 14.a represents the object of figure 11.b where the edges drawn in
thick lines were fused. Similarly figure 14.b represents the object of 10.a where the
faces displayed in solid surfaces were fused. In this case, the fusion operation gives an
object which is the boundary of the animation. In particular, if we have two animated
objects, we rapidly know if they cross the same point by calculating the intersection
of their boundaries. Imagine that the animated object is in a room, represented by a
parallelepiped. If we bind this parallelepiped and the boundary of the animated object,
we obtain the complementary of this object, i.e. the space in which the object never
goes.

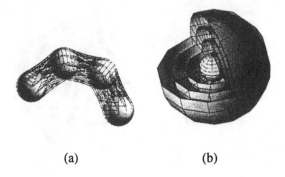

(a)   (b)

Figure 10: A hypersphere obtained by extrusion (a) and by scaling operation (b).

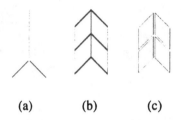

(a)   (b)   (c)

Figure 11: A chevron (a), its extrusion (b) and its 2-G-map (c).

When it is applied on the connecting faces, the fusion operation is the particular case of a general operation who allows to calculate the boundary of a manifold. In the case of objects obtained by extrusion, this fusion operation is more effective than the general operation. An n-D definition of this operation, applied to the G-maps, can be found in the article [15]. Figure 15.a shows an instance of 2-G-map and its boundary (a 1-G-map), and figure 15.b shows an instance of 3-G-map and its boundary (a 2-G-map).

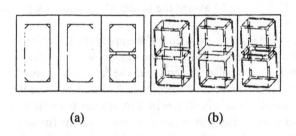

(a)   (b)

Figure 12: Fusion of two faces (a) and two volumes (b).

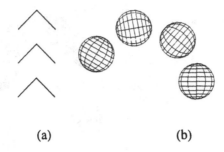

(a)   (b)

Figure 13: Fusion of connecting faces (a) and of connecting volumes (b).

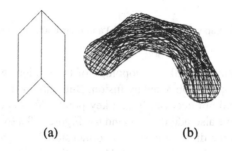

(a)   (b)

Figure 14: Fusion of invariable faces (a) and of invariable volumes (b).

4.4 Sequences of sections by a hyperplane

The operation of hyperplane splitting aims to generalize the fusion operation described in section 4.3. The section operation allows to extract 3-D objects at any date, even when the fusion operation allows only to extract 3-D objects at key-point. Figure 16.a presents a chevron extracted at halfway between the two firsts key-points of figure 11.b. Figure 16.b shows a 3-D sphere extracted between the second and the third key-points of figure 10.a. Figure 16.c (resp. 16.d) presents the projection of figure 16.a (resp. 16.b) along the z axis. Thus the cutting hyperplane is represented as a plane, which allows a better visualization of the section.

From the embedding point of view, the section operation consists in computing the intersection between a 4-D object and a hyperplane. From the topological point of view, it consists in closing the cutting G-map from the dimension 0 to the dimension 3. In order to close an n-G-map G at the dimension i, we have to compute the $(n-1)$-G-map G_i of its i-boundary, then we have to connect G_i to G by α_i. This closure is possible because by construction, G_i and the boundary of G are isomorphic. Figure 17.a presents the cutting 2-G-map of figure 11.b. Figure 17.b shows the 2-G-map closed at the dimension 0 (called G_0), by computing the 0-G-map of its 0-boundary (four darts) and connecting this 0-G-map to the cutting 2-G-map by α_0. Figure 17.c shows the 2-G-map closed at the dimension 1 (called G_1), that is G_0 plus its 1-boundary, and figure 17.d shows the 2-G-map closed at the dimension 2, that is G_1 plus its 2-boundary. This

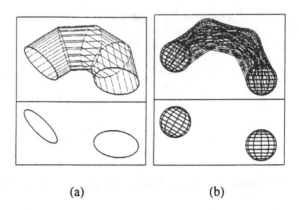

(a)   (b)

Figure 15: 1-G-map (a) and 2-G-map (b) and their boundaries in thick line.

last 2-boundary constitutes exactly the topology of the section, which is the same as the topology of the key-points obtained by fusion. But with this method, we can obtain sections at any date, and not necessarily at a key-point. We proceed in the same way with a 4-D object, but we also add the 3-boundary. Figures 18.a to figure 18.e show the 3-G-maps closed from the dimension 0 to the dimension 3, the initial 3-G-map is the cutting 3-G-map of figure 10.a. In practice [1], we directly compute the 3-boundary, without connecting it to the cutting 3-G-map.

The cutting hyperplane can be orthogonal to the time axis. The sequence of sections on figure 19 shows the evolution of a tetrahedron, and on figure 20 the evolution af a diapir [14]. In other respects, the cutting hyperplane can be non-orthogonal to the time axis. In this case, a single 4-D object can generate several animations. Figure 21 shows a number of animations obtained by the hypercube of figure 2. Figure 21.a presents the section by a hyperplane orthogonal to the time axis ($t = cte$). In figure 21.b, the section first meets a face ($x + t = cte$). Next in figure 21.c, the section first meets an edge ($x + y + t = cte$). Finally in figure 21.d, the section first intersects a vertex ($x + y + z + t = cte$). The set of the produced animations can cover an even wider range if the orientation of the cutting hyperplane could be modified over time.

Finally, if the sections are only displayed, we only mark the cutting darts in the initial G-map, and we stock the embedding of the intersection. On the contrary, if we wish to stock and manipulate the sections, we can create a G-map who contains the section. We can either choose to manually or automatically display successive seperate sections or simultaneously display them all.

4.5 Choosing a visualization mode

Classical geometric modellers allow often to represent three views (front view, side view and top view) of the 3-D objects. In 4-D, the equivalent visualization mode shows four different views of an object. With this method, we have a number of partial different views. But there is a depth missing on account of the lack of global view.

The complete visualization is ideal for the representation of the 4-D objects obtained

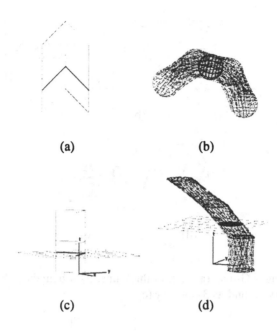

(a)   (b)

(c)   (d)

Figure 16: Section of an extruded chevron (a and b) and section of a hypersphere (c and d).

by extrusion. This is done by a more prominent visualization of the extrusion steps. But this mode can feign a space motion (translation, scaling operation) even when there is only a temporal motion. In such case the 4-D object provides a bad idea of the associated animation. Moreover, it may be impossible to simultaneously display wire frames and solid surfaces, for instance in the case of objects which are not obtained by extrusion. For such objects, complete visualization can only produce a rather confused vision of the 4-D object.

Finally, representing a sequence of sections offers a global vision of the animation. This mode is the necessary result of an animation-oriented modeller. But one of our goals is to apply operations on the 4-D object and to observe the consequences on the resulting animation, and this is not possible in the above mode. To do this, we must

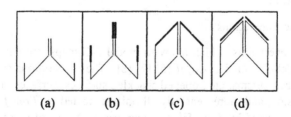

(a)   (b)   (c)   (d)

Figure 17: Cutting 2-G-map (a) and, in thick line, its 0-boundary (b), its 1-boundary (c) and its 2-boundary (d).

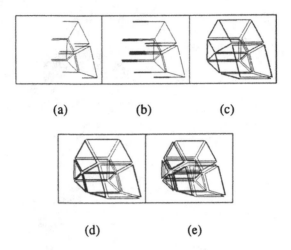

(a)　　　　　(b)　　　　　(c)

(d)　　　　　(e)

Figure 18: Cutting 3-G-map (a) and, in thick line, its 0-boundary (b), its 1-boundary (c), its 2-boundary (d) and its 3-bounary (e).

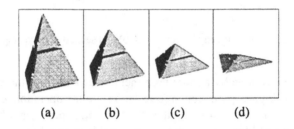

(a)　　　　(b)　　　　(c)　　　　(d)

Figure 19: Crushing of a tetrahedron.

simultaneously represent the section at a given time, and the 4-D object itself.

5 Building operations

5.1 3-D operations

5.1.1 Topological operations

3-D topological operations, which allow to model 2-G-maps, are developed in a G-maps-based modeller, called $Topofil$ [5] [7] [8]. These operations are primitives as spheres, tori, cubes, prisms, etc., opened shackled surfaces, surfaces obtained by revolution or extrusion, and more generally all objects created by $Topofil$. $STIGMA$ can read all files created by $Topofil$, and vice versa. A part of these operations are integrated in $STIGMA$. These objects, and the objects coming from $Topofil$ or other modellers, are embedded in a 3-D space. By default $STIGMA$ adds a nil time component. An other possibility is to use one of the three spatial components as the time component. In this case, the used spatial component becomes nil, and the object is

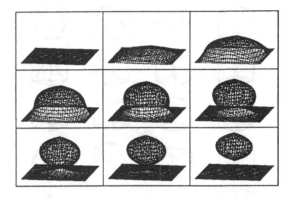

Figure 20: Evolution of a salt dome.

"flattened" in this component.

5.1.2 Embedding operations

Elementary operations, as translation, rotation, scaling operation, can be applied to three out of the four co-ordinates of the 4-D points. By default, the time component is ignored.

Moreover, a deformation operation based on the model $DOGME$ [3] is used to deform 3-D objects. At section 5.3, we show that this model can be applied to the 4-D objects, because it is an n-D model. This model deforms a set of points, the fact that these points are topologically structured has no importance. $DOGME$ has numerous applications, more particularly in animation [1] [4] [6].

$DOGME$ is a deformation model of an n-d space. A deformation $d : I\!\!R^n \longrightarrow I\!\!R^m$ is defined by the set of the n_c points of the space to deform, and the set of the n_c images of the deformed space. A point U of the initial space and a point $d(U)$ of the deformed space form a pair called a *constraint*. The shape of the deformed space is under the control of a function called *extrusion function*.

These functions define influence boxes who are centred on the beginning of the constraints, and determine the shape of the deformation. The boxes can be spherical (simple extrusion function) or parallelepipedical (simple product or tensor product). The general aspect of the deformation is determined by any function, generally a B-spline, a polynomial function, or sinusoidal function. Figure 22.a presents an instance of deformation by simple function, and figure 22.b shows an instance of deformation by simple product.

In a 3-D space, the interest of this model is to allow a large range of deformations. We obtain precise deformations, because they satisfy the constraints, which are easy to define. In a 4-D space, $DOGME$ is a powerful tool which allows to simultaneously modify the four co-ordinates of 4-D points, including the time co-ordinate. It allows to send a part of the points "in the future" or "in the past" [1]. For numerous objects, the deformations are computed in real time, as the user interactively modifies a constraint.

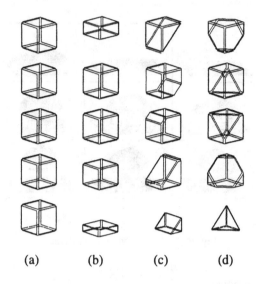

Figure 21: Number of successive sections of a hypercube.

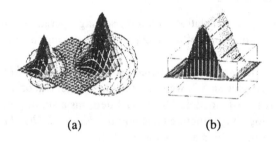

Figure 22: Deformed grid with a simple function (a) and simple product (b).

5.2 Operations increasing the number of dimensions

5.2.1 The particular case of the extrusion operation

Among the operations increasing the number of dimensions we focused on extrusions. We can extrude objects with an open trajectory, or with a closed trajectory. A closed trajectory allows a single 3-D object to be divided in several objects (at an intermediate time), and to be merged back in one object.

From a topological point of view, the extrusion produces an $(n + 1)$-G-map from an n-G-map $(0 \leq n \leq 2)$. Figure 23 shows a hypercube obtained from a single dart, by successive extrusions along a segment. Figure 24 presents the extrusion of a shackled surface along a linear trajectory composed of 10 segments. These two types of extrusion are particular cases, corresponding to a linear trajectory. They are frequently used. This is why the trajectory is not an explicitly polygonal line, but only an origin, a direction, a number and a size of extrusion step. Another particular case of extrusion corresponding to a circular trajectory. This operation is called revolution. Figure 25.a presents a hypertorus obtained by the revolution of a 3-D sphere. Figure 25.b shows a section sequence of this hypertorus. In this instance, the 3-D sphere is split into two parts, then the two spheres merge back into one at the end of the animation.

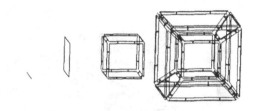

Figure 23: Hypercube obtained by successive extrusions.

Figure 24: Extrusion of a cube with rotation and scale controled by a B-spline.

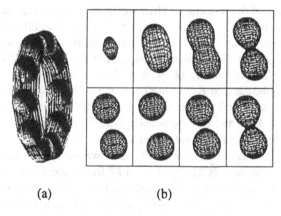

(a)   (b)

Figure 25: Hypertorus (a) and sections sequence (b).

5.2.2 The general case of the extrusion operation

In the general case, the extrusion trajectory is any polygonal line. Moreover the extrusion characterized by a torsion angle γ. To do this, we apply a rotation of angle γ to the extruded object at each key-point. We also associate a scale function with the extrusion. In order to do this, we apply a scale at the extruded object at each key-point, the scale factor is given by the scale function. Figure 26.a presents a 3-D screw, obtained by applying an important scale factor. The diameter changes are under the control of the scale function. Figure 26.b shows an animated spring. The size changes are obtained by the application of a scale to a single co-ordinate.

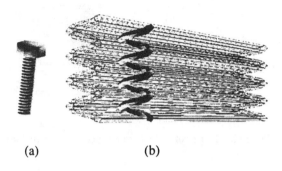

(a)   (b)

Figure 26: A 3-D screw (a) and a compressed spring (b).

The extrusion along any 3-D path already exists in $Topofil$ or other modellers. In 4-D, other techniques are necessary in order to compute rotation angles and planes associated with each extrusion step. In $STIGMA$, these rotation computations are implemented as a part of the extrusion process.

We can interactively draw a 4-D poloygonal line to define the extrusion. This line defines a space-time path between the initial 3-D object and the final 3-D object. The i-th 3-D object is obtained by the translation of the $(i - 1)$-th 3-D object along the $(i - 1)$-th segment of the trajectory. Then we apply a rotation to the i-th 3-D object. The rotation angle is half the angle formed by the $(i - 1)$-th and the i-th segments. The rotation plane is the plane which is orthogonal to the plane enclosing both segments. This plane is unique for the following reason. Let L_n be an n-D vector space, and L_k a k-D vector subspace of L_n ($k \leq n$). Then, there exists a unique $(n - k)$-D vector subspace orthogonal to L_k. In our case, in a 4-D vector space, we can find two independant vectors $\overrightarrow{u}$ and $\overrightarrow{v}$ that define a plane Q, who is orthognal to the plane defined by the $(i - 1)$-th and i-th segments only if these segments are not collinear. If these segments are collinear, no rotation is carry out.

To carry out the rotation around the Q plane, we use a reference transfer matrix, determined by the four vectors $\overrightarrow{v_1}$, $\overrightarrow{v_2}$, $\overrightarrow{v_3}$ and $\overrightarrow{v_4}$ from a local basis of Q. This change allows rotations around one of the six orthotropic planes. Let P be a point of the object which we want to rotate, and P' the orthogonal projection of P on Q. We determine two vectors $\overrightarrow{v_1}$ and $\overrightarrow{v_2}$ in Q. The vector $\overrightarrow{v_3}$, carried by the $P'P$ line, is orthogonal to $\overrightarrow{v_1}$ and $\overrightarrow{v_2}$. We obtain vector $\overrightarrow{v_4}$ by computing the scalar product of $\overrightarrow{v_1}$, $\overrightarrow{v_2}$ and $\overrightarrow{v_3}$. Figure 27 represents this situation. The $\{\overrightarrow{v_1}, \overrightarrow{v_2}, \overrightarrow{v_3}, \overrightarrow{v_4}\}$ system forms a basis. Then we build the reference transfer matrix M:

$$v_1 = \begin{pmatrix} x_1 \\ y_1 \\ z_1 \\ t_1 \end{pmatrix}, v_2 = \begin{pmatrix} x_2 \\ y_2 \\ z_2 \\ t_2 \end{pmatrix}, v_3 = \begin{pmatrix} x_3 \\ y_3 \\ z_3 \\ t_3 \end{pmatrix},$$

$$v_4 = \begin{pmatrix} x_4 \\ y_4 \\ z_4 \\ t_4 \end{pmatrix}, M = \begin{pmatrix} x_1 & x_2 & x_3 & x_4 \\ y_1 & y_2 & y_3 & y_4 \\ z_1 & z_2 & z_3 & z_4 \\ t_1 & t_2 & t_3 & t_4 \end{pmatrix}$$

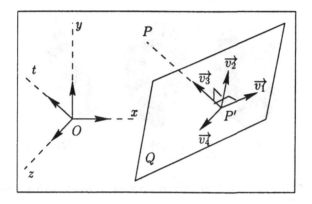

Figure 27: Computing of reference transfer.

The matrix product of P and M is the reference transfer matrix, putting the Q plane on the xy plane. The last step consists in realizing the rotation by building the rotation matrix around the xy plane. We can also adjust the size of the intermediate volumes in order to compensate the rotation effect. To do this, we apply a local scale to these volumes, the scale factor computed from the rotation angle. Figure 28.a represents the extrusion of a segment without compensation, figure 28.b the same extrusion with compensation.

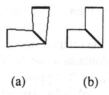

(a)   (b)

Figure 28: Scale to compensate the rotation.

5.3   4-D operations

5.3.1   Topological operations

In 4-D as in 3-D, we have numerous primitives at our disposal, in order to facilitate the construction of more complex objects. We can create some 4-D objects by the extrusion of 3-D primitives. $STIGMA$ henceforth allows to directly create 4-D objects. One of these primitives is the hypercube on figure 2.b. $STIGMA$ also allows other primitives, such as tori, prisms, tetrahedra, pyramids, open shackled volumes, 4-D analogous of 3-D open shackled surfaces. Figure 29 represents some primitives.

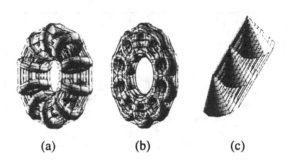

(a)   (b)   (c)

Figure 29: Two sights of the revolution af a torus (a and b), and hypercone (c).

5.3.2   Embedding operations

As in 3-D, we have at our disposal translations, rotations, scales and the deformation model $DOGME$. In this case, $DOGME$ is used in 4-D to apply space-time deformations. These operations are identical to their 3-D counterparts, apart from the rotation. This is why we detail only the rotation operation, also mentioned in section 5.2.2.

The 4-D rotation is executed around a plane. In an n-D space, the rotation is executed around an axis, that is an $(n-2)$-D subspace : the axis is a point in a 2-D space, a line in a 3-D space, and a plane in a 4-D space. In addition, each point turns in a plane, whatever the dimension of the space may be. In this way, each non-invariant point (i.e. point who does not belong to the rotation axis) describes a circle c included in a plane orthogonal to the rotation axis.

Let P be a point concerned by the rotation, and P' the orthogonal projection of P on the rotation axis. Whatever the dimension may be, P is transformed along the circle C of center P' and radius PP'. On the 2-D plane, C belongs to the plane. In 3-D, C belongs to the plane which is orthogonal to the axis and passes by P. In 4-D, C belongs to the plane which is orthogonal to the rotation plane and passes by P. In section 5.2.2, we have seen that this plane is unique.

Thus the 4-D rotation is defined around the six orthotropic planes xy, xz, xt, yz, yt and zt. The rotation of a point P is obtained by multiplying P and one of the six rotation matrices which are deduced from the 3-D rotation matrices. The following instance presents a rotation around the xz plane:

$$\begin{pmatrix} x' \\ y' \\ z' \\ t' \\ w' \end{pmatrix} = \begin{pmatrix} x \\ y \\ z \\ t \\ w \end{pmatrix} \cdot \begin{pmatrix} 1 & 0 & 0 & 0 & 0 \\ 0 & cos\theta & 0 & sin\theta & 0 \\ 0 & 0 & 1 & 0 & 0 \\ 0 & -sin\theta & 0 & cos\theta & 0 \\ 0 & 0 & 0 & 0 & 1 \end{pmatrix}$$

$STIGMA$ allows to carry out these rotations. It may be a local rotation around a plane which passes through the barycentre of the selected object, or a global rotation around a plane which passes through the origin, or a rotation around any plane obtained with a reference transfer (see section 5.2.2). $STIGMA$ can represent the rotation plane and put to the fore the points that the rotation leaves invariant. Thus we can actually see the rotation of a 4-D object around a plane. Figure 30 represents the rotation of a hypercube around plane xy. We use the complete visualization with a scaling operation to represent the hypercube. The rotation of this hypercube around the xy plane defines a vertical motion. The illusion of volume modification results from the scaling operation used in the visualization.

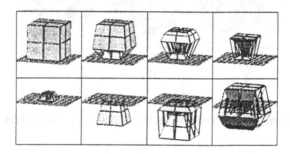

Figure 30: Rotation of a hypercube around the xy plane.

6   Conclusion

We have described the construction and deformation of 3-D and 4-D objects, the operations increasing the number of dimensions as extrusions, operations decreasing this number as sections, boundary computing, volume fusion. These operations constitute a core for a 4-D geometric modeller, which does not set any limitation on the set of possible 4-D objects, and therefore on the resulting 3-D animations. Figure 31.a presents a five-hole torus, and figure 31.b the associated animation, with several splitting and merging 3-D spheres and n-hole tori.

Current work deals with the study and the implementation of numerous higher level operations, and more animation-dedicated operations, in order to better control the shape and the structure of 3-D animations. We are working on an extension of the extrusion operation, in order to control the trajectory by a graph. For this, we associate several modelling operations to solve the problem of the blend between the differents parts of the extruded object, at the nodes of the graph. This operation will allow to

124

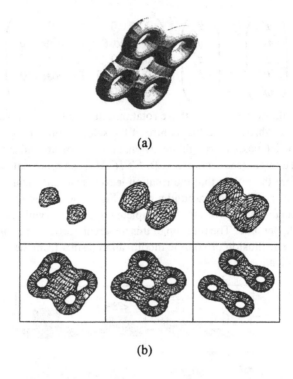

(a)

(b)

Figure 31: Five-hole torus (a) and its associated animation (b).

precisely control the number and the exact date of the merging and the splitting. We also study the concatenation of animations, and the creation of animations allowing to concatenate two given animations. The realization of these blends requires the study of 4-D objects which could transform a 3-D object in another 3-D object with another topology (variation in sort and/or adjustability). It is also necessary to design higher level embedding operations, in order to increase the control of the 3-D objects' shape, and design operations to manipulate the cutting hyperplane. Current work consists of a thorough study and implementation of these operations in order to achieve an easy control of the entire process of 3-D animation by 4-D object construction, which, in turn, is necessary for the achievement of a wide range of animations.

Acknoledgements

Many thanks to Arash Habibi for his help to write this article in English.

References

1. AUBERT F., BECHMANN D., Animation by Deformation of Space-Time Objects, Eurographics'97, Budapest, Hungary, 1997.

2. BAUMGART B.G., A Polyhedron Representation for Computer Vision, Proc. AFIPS Nat. Conf. 44, pp 589-596, 1975.

3. BORREL P., BECHMANN D., Deformation of n-dimensional objects, Intern. Journal of Comp. Geometry and Appl. vol. 1, n4, pp 427-453, 1991.

4. BECHMANN D., DUBREUIL N., Animation through space and time based on a space deformation model, The journal of visualisation and computer animation, vol. 4, n3, pp 165-184, 1993.

5. BERTRAND Y., DUFOURD J.-F., Algebraic Specification of a 3D-Modeller Based on Hypermaps, Computer vision, graphical model, and image processing, vol. 56, n1, pp 29-60, 1994.

6. BECHMANN D., DUBREUIL N., Order controlled Free-Form Animation, The Journal of Visualization and Computer Animation,Wiley, vol. 5, n1, pp 11-32, 1995.

7. BERTRAND Y., DUFOURD J.-F., FRANCON J., LIENHARDT P., Modélisation volumique à base topologique, actes du MICAD 92, Paris, février 1992.

8. BERTRAND Y., Topofil : un modeleur interactif d'objets 3D à base topologique, to appear in TSI.

9. COQUILLART S., JANCENE P., Animated free-form deformation: an interactive animation technique, Computer Graphics (SIGGRAPH'91), vol 25, pp 23-26, 1991.

10. DUBREUIL N., LIENHARDT P., un modèle d'ani-mation basé sur les ensembles simpliciaux cubiques 4D, Rapport de recherche IRCOM-SIC, Poitiers, 1997.

11. FOUSSE A., BERTRAND Y., DUFOURD J.-F., FRANCON J., RODRIGUES D., Localisation des points d'un maillage généré en vue de calculs en différences finies, Journées "Modélisation du sous-sol", Orléans, février 1997 (Rapport de recherche 96-21, Université Louis Pasteur, Strasbourg).

12. HSU W.-M., HUGHES J.-F., KAUFMAN H., direct manipulation on free-form deformation, SIGGRAPH'92, ACM Comp. Graph., vol. 26, n2, pp 177-184, 1992.

13. JACQUES A., Constellations et graphes topologiques, in Combinatorial Theory and Applications, Budapest, Hungary, pp 657-673, 1970.

14. LIENHARDT P., BERTRAND Y., BECHMANN D., 4D-Modelling with G-maps and *DOGME*, Gocad Meeting, Nancy, France, 1997.

15. LIENHARDT P., Subdivisions of N-Dimensional Spaces and N-Dimensional Generalized Maps, Proc. 5-th Annual A.C.M. Symposium on Computational Geometry, Saarbrücken, Germany, pp 228-236, 1989.

16. LIENHARDT P., Topological models for boundary representation: a comparison with n-dimensional generalized maps, C.A.D., vol. 23, n1, pp 59-82, 1991.

17. LAZARUS F., VERROUST, A., Metamorphosis of Cylinder-like Objects, The journal of visualization and computer animation, vol 8, n3, pp 131-146, 1997.

18. ROSSIGNAC J., KAUL A., AGRELS and BIBs: metamorphosis as a Bezier curve in the space of polyedra, Eurographic's 94, Oslo, Norway, pp 179-194, 1994.

19. SEDERBERG T.-W., PARRY S.-R., Free-Form Deformation of Solid Geometric Models, Proc. Siggraph 86, Dallas, USA, pp 151-160, 1986.

20. TERRAZ O., LIENHARDT P., A study of basic tools for simulating metamorphoses of subdivided 2D and 3D objects. Applications to the internal growing of wood and to the simulation of the growing of fishes, 6th Eurographics Workshop on animation and simulation, Maastricht, Netherlands, in Computer Animation and Simulation'95 (D. Terzopoulos et D. Thalmann eds, springer), pp. 104-129, 1995.

21. WEILER K., Edge-Based Data Structures for Solid Modeling in Curved-Surface Environments, IEEE Comp. Graphics and Appl., vol. 5, n1, pp 21-40, 1985.

22. WEILER K., Boundary Graph Operators for Non-Manifold Geometric Modeling Topology Representation, IFIP Conf. on Geometric Modeling for CAD Applications, Elsevier, North-Holland, pp 37-66, 1988.

SpringerEurographics

Martin Göbel,

Jürgen Landauer, Ulrich Lang,

Matthias Wapler (eds.)

Virtual Environments '98

Proceedings of the Eurographics Workshop
in Stuttgart, Germany, June 16–18, 1998

1998. VIII, 335 pages. 206 partly coloured figures.
Softcover DM 128,–, öS 896,–
ISBN 3-211-83233-5. Eurographics

Ten years after Virtual Environment research started with NASA's VIEW project, these techniques are now exploited in industry to speed up product development cycles, to ensure higher product quality, and to encourage early training on and for new products. Especially the automotive industry, but also the oil and gas industry are driving the use of these techniques in their works.

The papers in this volume reflect all the different tracks of the workshop: reviewed technical papers as research contributions, summaries on panels of VE applications in the automotive, the medical, the telecommunication and the geoscience field, a panel discussing VEs as the future workspace, invited papers from experts reporting from VEs for entertainment industry, for media arts, for supercomputing and productivity enhancement. Short industrial case studies, reporting very briefly from ongoing industrial activities complete this state of the art snapshot.

Dirk Bartz (ed.)

Visualization in Scientific Computing '98

Proceedings of the Eurographics
Workshop in Blaubeuren, Germany,
April 20–22, 1998

1998. VII, 151 pages. 82 figures.
Softcover DM 85,–, öS 595,–
ISBN 3-211-83209-2. Eurographics

In twelve selected papers common problems in scientific visualization are discussed: adaptive and multi-resolution methods, feature extraction, flow visualization, and visualization quality. Four papers focus on aspects of mesh reduction, mesh compression, and increasing the quality of the resulting mesh. Two extentions on particle tracing are presented as well as a paper on the simulation of material transport. Two papers are on feature extraction in dynamics systems and on the accuracy of algorithmic extracted features. Three papers focus on stereoscopic volume rendering, on the visualization of atomic collision cascades and of quality of visualization systems in general.

SpringerWienNewYork

Sachsenplatz 4-6, P.O.Box 89, A-1201 Wien, Fax +43-1-330 24 26, e-mail: order@springer.at, Internet: http://www.springer.at
New York, NY 10010, 175 Fifth Avenue • D-14197 Berlin, Heidelberger Platz 3 • Tokyo 113, 3-13, Hongo 3-chome, Bunkyo-ku

SpringerEurographics

George Drettakis,

Nelson Max (eds.)

Rendering Techniques '98

Proceedings of the Eurographics
Workshop in Vienna, Austria,
June 29–July 1, 1998

1998. XI, 339 pages. 231 partly coloured figures.
Softcover DM 118,–, öS 826,–
ISBN 3-211-83213-0. Eurographics

Some of the best current research on realistic rendering is included in this volume. It emphasizes the current "hot topics" in this field: image based rendering, and efficient local and global-illumination calculations. In the first of these areas, there are several contributions on real-world model acquisition and display, on using image-based techniques for illumination and on efficient ways to parameterize and compress images or light fields, as well as on clever uses of texture and compositing hardware to achieve image warping and 3D surface textures. In global and local illumination, there are contributions on extending the techniques beyond diffuse reflections, to include specular and more general angle dependent reflection functions, on efficiently representing and approximating these reflection functions, on representing light sources and on approximating visibility and shadows. Finally, there are two contributions on how to use knowledge about human perception to concentrate the work of accurate rendering only where it will be noticed, and a survey of computer graphics techniques used in the production of a feature length computer-animated film with full 3D characters.

Panos Markopoulos,

Peter Johnson (eds.)

Design, Specification and Verification of Interactive Systems '98

Proceedings of the Eurographics
Workshop in Abingdon, U.K.,
June 3–5, 1998

1998. IX, 325 pages. 119 figures.
Softcover approx. DM 118,–, öS 826,–
ISBN 3-211-83212-2. Eurographics

Does modelling, formal or otherwise, have a role to play in designing interactive systems? A proliferation of interactive devices and technologies are used in an ever increasing diversity of contexts and combinations in professional and every-day life. This development poses a significant challenge to modelling approaches used for the design of interactive systems. The papers in this volume discuss a range of modelling approaches, the representations they use, the strengths and weaknesses of their associated specification and analysis techniques and their role in supporting the design of interactive systems.

 SpringerWienNewYork

Sachsenplatz 4-6, P.O.Box 89, A-1201 Wien, Fax +43-1-330 24 26, e-mail: order@springer.at, Internet: http://www.springer.at
New York, NY 10010, 175 Fifth Avenue • D-14197 Berlin, Heidelberger Platz 3 • Tokyo 113, 3-13, Hongo 3-chome, Bunkyo-ku